Making Sense of

GOD'S PLAN FOR HUMANITY

AN EASY-TO-UNDERSTAND GUIDE TO DISPENSATIONALISM

Dr. Douglas C. Bozung

DISPENSATIONAL
PUBLISHING HOUSE, INC.

All Scripture quotations, unless otherwise indicated,
are taken from the New King James Version®.
Copyright © 1982 by Thomas Nelson. Used by permission. All rights reserved.

Scripture quotations marked NASB are taken from the New American Standard Bible®,
Copyright © 1960, 1962, 1963, 1968, 1971, 1972, 1973, 1975, 1977, 1995 by The Lockman Foundation. Used by permission. (www.Lockman.org)

Scripture quotations marked (ESV) are from the ESV® Bible (The Holy Bible, English Standard Version®), copyright © 2001 by Crossway, a publishing ministry of Good News Publishers. Used by permission. All rights reserved.

Scripture quotations marked (NIV) are taken from the Holy Bible,
New International Version®, NIV®. Copyright © 1973, 1978, 1984, 2011 by Biblica, Inc.™
Used by permission of Zondervan. All rights reserved worldwide. www.zondervan.com
The "NIV" and "New International Version" are trademarks
registered in the United States Patent and Trademark Office by Biblica, Inc.™

Scripture quotations marked KJV are taken from the King James Version of the Bible.

Printed in the United States of America
First Edition, First Printing, 2017
ISBN: 978-1-945774-04-1

Dispensational Publishing House, Inc.
220 Paseo del Pueblo Norte
Taos, NM 87571

www.dispensationalpublishing.com

Ordering Information: Quantity sales. Special discounts are available on quantity purchases by churches, associations, and others. For details, contact the publisher at the address above.

Orders by U.S. trade bookstores and wholesalers. Please contact the publisher:
Tel: (844) 321-4202

1 2 3 4 5 6 7 8 9 10

To Rev. George Kolar, Sr., now with the Lord,

who first introduced me to

the concept of dispensationalism,

I affectionately dedicate this work.

Table of Contents

Chapter 7

Chapter 8

Chapter 9

Appendix 1

Appendix 2

Endnotes

ENDORSEMENTS

"Dispensationalism is one of the most misrepresented and caricatured approaches to the Bible within the evangelical world. *Making Sense of God's Plan for Humanity*, as the subtitle suggests, is an easy guide to understand dispensationalism. Doug has made the simplicity of this approach available for the average Bible reader. This should be a work that is often used."

Dr. Michael Stallard
Moderator of the Council on Dispensational Hermeneutics;
director of international ministries for The Friends of Israel Gospel Ministry, Inc.

"With this volume, Doug has performed a wonderful service for all who are interested to understand what dispensationalists actually believe. In a charitable, pastoral style, he provides a helpful overview of the main tenets of dispensationalism, clear and accessible for all readers. I am delighted to recommend this book to enhance your own study of the Scriptures."

Dr. Samuel Harbin
Chair of the Bible and theology department,
Lancaster Bible College, Lancaster, Pa.

"An excellent and very readable treatment of the subject of dispensationalism....
I highly recommend this book to all."

Dr. Renald Showers
Former professor of Bible at Lancaster Bible College,
Moody Bible Institute and Cairn University;
former author and Bible teacher for The Friends of Israel Gospel Ministry, Inc.

FOREWORD

Dispensationalism has been hailed as the secret to unlocking the meaning of God's Word . . . and condemned as heresy. And yet, in spite of strong feelings on both sides, there is one thing champions and critics alike often share in common—they don't fully comprehend what dispensationalism is all about. Dr. Doug Bozung has set out to solve that problem!

Several good books on dispensationalism have appeared in the past. Perhaps the best is *Dispensationalism Today* by the late Dr. Charles Ryrie. He did an excellent job of defining and defending dispensationalism. Unfortunately, his book has not been widely read outside the college and seminary classroom. In this new work, Doug Bozung brings the logic and clarity of *Dispensationalism Today* to a larger audience.

Making Sense of God's Plan for Humanity is designed to help ordinary followers of Jesus make sense of the Bible. It's written to be understood by someone attending a Sunday school class or Bible study. The writing style is clear and simple but not simplistic. The discussion questions at the end of each chapter help individuals and groups review and reflect on the material.

In an age when Bible study is often reduced to little more than a babble of voices sharing "what the passage means to me," Doug provides a healthy reminder that the Bible is intended to be interpreted literally. What matters most is what God meant when He superintended the writing of the Bible, not what we might like it to mean. Understanding dispensational distinctives allows an individual to follow the unfolding of God's Word through the different ages.

So who should read this book? Pastors and teachers should read it to review and reinforce the principles of solid interpretation they learned in school. And anyone who wants to be a serious student of the Bible should read it to understand how to "rightly divide the word of truth."

Dr. Charles H. Dyer
Professor-at-large of Bible, Moody Bible Institute, Chicago,
and host of *The Land and the Book* radio program, Moody Radio;
associate pastor, Grace Bible Church, Sun City, Ariz.

PREFACE

Many fine expositions of the teachings of dispensationalism have been written in recent years, some of which are referenced in this present volume. For the most part, such works were written for a more academic audience of professors, pastors and serious students of the Bible. By contrast, this book is intended for a lay audience that has little or no familiarity with the concepts of dispensationalism. Much of the content in the following pages comes from my preaching and teaching ministry at Christian Fellowship Church in New Holland, Pa., where I have been privileged to serve for the past eight years as teaching pastor. Footnotes as well as appendices at the end of this book provide a more in-depth discussion of particular topics as well as further resources for study.

The reader is encouraged to carefully examine the introduction, which is designed to explain the meaning of the terms *dispensation* and *dispensationalism*. Following this crucial introductory chapter, the various dispensations found in the Bible are described in chronological order. The concluding chapters deal with common objections to dispensationalism as well as a description of the practical value of the dispensational approach to the Bible.

This book is also intended for use in a group or classroom setting. Discussion questions at the end of each chapter can be used for group interaction, classroom instruction or personal enrichment. Also, the numerous Bible references used throughout this book to support or illustrate certain points can supplement the study of Scripture in a group or personal setting.

This brief volume is not intended to be a robust defense of dispensational teachings, though the first appendix provides a detailed argument for the doctrine of a pretribulational rapture. Rather, my intention is to provide understanding through straightforward explanation and illustration. For thorough defenses, the reader is directed to the many referenced sources.

I was first exposed to the teachings of dispensationalism during the formative years of my Christian life. More than 40 years later, I find them to be the best explanation of the truths of God's Word and a valuable aid to my ministry as a pastor and professor. I trust that you also will benefit greatly from the teachings of dispensationalism as presented in this basic introduction.

Many thanks to my family and friends who assisted me in the production of this book through thoughtful feedback and suggestions for improvement, including my brother, Chris, who supplied the essence of the chart on page 25. And very special thanks to my wife, Alicia, who encouraged me throughout the many hours of writing and editing.

To God alone be the glory!

Douglas C. Bozung
March 13, 2017

INTRODUCTION
TRYING TO MAKE SENSE OF IT ALL

When we think about what God is doing in the world today, we may likely scratch our heads. Many times our world seems chaotic and out of control. The behavior of so many, even some who profess to believe in God, seems quite contrary to what we believe God desires to see in our lives. We may assume God has a plan and purpose, and we may even believe that He is ultimately in control of all that happens. Yet many events, especially those that directly impact our lives, seem to deny these assumptions and beliefs.

Can the Bible give us any insight here? Indeed, it can. Rightly understood, the Bible clearly explains God's plans and purposes for humanity as well as how He has dealt with mankind from the beginning of time. The Bible also informs us as to what God is doing today, what his expectations are for his children and what He plans to do in the future.

But the key phrase here is *rightly understood.* Many in our world today, even some who profess to be devoted followers of Jesus, insist that the Bible can be understood in many ways, and that no one way of interpretation is right. They say what the Bible means to you personally is what is most important, regardless of what someone else may think or believe. This very popular point of view[1] insists that no one system of belief or way of looking at the world is superior to, or more *truthful,* than any other. What is *true* for you may not be *true* for someone else, and vice versa. In other words, truth is in the eye of the beholder.

However, this way of looking at truth creates great confusion. Who is right and who is wrong? If everyone is *right*, what do we do when two or more *true* beliefs contradict one another? When such an approach to truth is applied to the interpretation of the Bible, great confusion also results. Rather than leading us to a satisfactory understanding of the teachings of the Bible and of what God is really doing in our world, such an approach to the Bible largely leads one to despair of ever understanding the Bible correctly. Unfortunately, this perspective has led many to abandon the search for truth through the Bible altogether.

Toward a Better Way to Understand the Bible

Thankfully, there is a better and more satisfying way to understand the Bible. That way is based upon what may seem to be a very obvious truth or principle. This principle is the assumption that *a writer had something specific in mind when he wrote what he did.* For example, if someone leaves a note that says, "Out to lunch," we may reasonably assume that someone is having their lunch in another location. Likewise, when the Bible says, "all have sinned" (Rom. 3:23), we can again reasonably assume that the writer is expressing the view that everyone on the earth has sinned.

Admittedly, these two examples are fairly simple and straight-forward. But this principle holds true no matter how complex the writing or piece of literature may be. Sometimes a writer may use certain artistic forms of expression, such as a poem or a Psalm, to express his or her thoughts. However, the principle still holds that the writer had something specific in mind when the words contained in such types of literature were penned.

This fundamental principle is the basis for what is known as *literal interpretation*. Literal interpretation means that the piece of literature in question is to be understood in accordance with the normal rules of grammar and the universally accepted meanings of words as expressed by the writer. In other words, unless the writer indicates otherwise, we take him at his word. This does not mean that a writer cannot use word plays or figures of speech. For example, when Jesus said, "I am the light of the world" (John 8:12), no one imagines when reading these words that Jesus was claiming to be a cosmic light bulb.[2] Or when John the Baptist observed Jesus approaching him and said, "Behold the Lamb of God!" (John 1:36), no one thinks he saw a white, fluffy four-legged animal. Rather, literal interpretation recognizes that, just like with many other great works of literature, the authors of the Bible sometimes employed creative and artistic ways of communicating, which can and should be recognized as such. However, in most instances, the Bible can be understood in a very straightforward manner, just like most human communication.[3]

The Basis for Dispensationalism

So literal interpretation is the basis for properly understanding the Bible. It is also the basis for the approach to the Bible known as dispensationalism. That is, the term *dispensationalism* refers in part to the conviction that the Bible should be interpreted literally and no other way. This also means we should not employ literal interpretation in one section of the Bible and then abandon it in another section of the Bible. Rather, *all* of the Bible is to be interpreted by the same rules of interpretation.[4]

Now, I can imagine someone objecting at this point to this interpretive approach by observing, for example, that the book of Revelation is filled with many unusual figures of speech and symbols, some of which are notoriously difficult to interpret. However, while it is true that some of the imagery found in the book of Revelation is challenging to identify or interpret correctly, we must still insist that our interpretive approach to that fascinating book of the Bible be the same approach we use in any other book of the Bible. The problem is that once we abandon literal interpretation, then the meaning of the text of Scripture is at the mercy of the individual interpreter, and we will find ourselves right back in a sea of confusion.

As will be seen in the course of this book, this aspect of dispensationalism is also crucial to understanding other aspects of dispensationalism. In fact, according to most dispensationalists, literal interpretation is one of the chief characteristics of dispensationalism that differentiates it from other approaches to the Bible.[5] Another way to say this is that *the dispensational understanding of the Bible is governed by the consistent use of literal interpretation throughout Scripture.* This approach is in contrast to other systems of interpretation that tend to abandon literal interpretation at certain points, especially when dealing with Old Testament prophecies concerning the nation of Israel. When this happens, rather than being interpreted literally, certain Old Testament passages are reinterpreted or *spiritualized* in a manner that removes them from their original context and audience in order that they can be applied to a present-day audience. As a result, promises originally given to the people of Israel by God and covenants originally made with the leaders and nation of Israel are either voided completely or else reassigned in a *spiritual* form to the church today.

Dispensationalism Defined

But what exactly is dispensationalism? To answer that question, I would like to begin by offering an illustration or an analogy from the relationship between parents and children. When children are very young, they depend upon their parents for everything: what to eat, what to wear, when to sleep, when to bathe, etc. But as children grow older they begin to assume more of these responsibilities for themselves. They begin to exercise greater independence from—and, in some cases, rebel against—their parents. By the time they reach late adolescence, most children are functioning in virtual independence from their parents. Throughout all this time they never cease to be their parents' children. However, their relationship to their parents changes over time. That is, parents and children do not relate to one another during the period of adolescence in the same way they related to one another during the period of infancy.

In a similar way, as we examine the course of human history, we see that the way God has related to humanity over time has changed. For example, in the very beginning, there was a period of human *infancy*, when humankind, represented by our first parents, Adam and Eve, had no knowledge of evil and sin. As such, they enjoyed a very intimate relationship with God. However, once Adam and Eve succumbed to temptation and sinned by disobeying God, their relationship with God changed radically, resulting in their expulsion from God's presence (Gen. 3:22–24). This changed relationship led to a new and different way in which God related to Adam and Eve and their posterity.

Very broadly defined, *dispensationalism is the belief that God has related to people in the course of human history in unique ways*. Each of these unique historical relationships between God and people is called a *dispensation*. The late Dr. Charles Ryrie defined dispensations as, "God's distinctive and different administrations in directing the affairs of the world."[6] And Dr. Renald Showers defines a dispensation as,

"A particular way of God's administering His rule over the world as He progressively works out His purpose for world history."[7]

For example, the initial period described above in which Adam and Eve enjoyed an intimate relationship with God is known as the *dispensation of innocence.* The period of history in which God related to people through the nation of Israel is called the *dispensation of law*, primarily because the law of Moses was God's means of defining and conducting their relationship with him. The present dispensation is known as the *dispensation of grace*, in which God relates to and reveals Himself to the world through the church, which Jesus promised He would one day "build" (Matt. 16:18). This dispensation is so named because the *fullness* of God's grace toward sinful humanity has been made evident through the Person of Jesus Christ in ways never before seen in history. As the Apostle Paul puts it: "The grace of God that brings salvation has appeared to all men" (Tit. 2:11).

Most dispensationalists recognize the existence of seven dispensations in the course of history: innocence (Gen. 1–3), conscience (Gen. 4–8), government (Gen. 9–11), promise (Gen. 12–Ex. 18), law (Ex. 19–Acts 1), grace (Acts 2–Rev. 19) and kingdom (Rev. 20).[8] These designations, as well as their unique characteristics, will be explored in greater detail in ensuing chapters.

Scriptural Illustrations of the Concept of Dispensationalism

The analogy involving parents and children has some affinity with the Greek word *oikonomia*, which is translated as *dispensation* in certain English versions of the New Testament (see, for example, the King James Version of 1 Cor. 9:17; Eph. 1:10, 3:2; and Col. 1:25). In the first-century world, an *oikonomia* (literally "house law") referred to the management of a household by a steward, or *oikonomos*. Thus, we could say that, "Dispensationalism views the world as a household run by God."[9]

One well-respected dictionary of the Greek New Testament defines an *oikonomia* as, "A plan which involves a set of arrangements (referring . . . to God's plan for bringing salvation to mankind within the course of history)."[10] Thus, Paul writes that one of his responsibilities as an apostle was "to bring to light for everyone what is the plan [*oikonomia*] of the mystery hidden for ages in God who created all things" (Eph. 3:9, ESV[11]). This particular usage of *oikonomia* by Paul is very similar to what is meant by a dispensation. That is, Paul speaks of his responsibility to make known a new *plan*, or arrangement, between God and people through faith in Jesus Christ.

Another illustration of how the relationship or arrangement between God and people has changed throughout human history is the difference between the way a child of God in Israel (during the *dispensation of law*) and child of God today (in the *dispensation of grace*) relate to God. During Old Testament times, an Israelite could never directly approach God. Rather, all interaction with God had to be conducted by means of a special order of priests, who were ordained by God to offer sacrifices to God on behalf of the nation. A believer in Christ today, however, can "come boldly to the throne of grace" (Heb. 4:16) and thereby enter into the very presence of God. This is made possible because of the intercessory ministry of the one high priest, Jesus Christ (Heb. 4:16; cf. Rom. 8:34; 1 John 2:2). Indeed, every true believer in Christ is called a *priest* (1 Pet. 2:9; Rev. 1:6).

Now, admittedly, most Christians, including most non-dispensationalists, would agree with the relational and historical changes noted in this example. That is, virtually everyone recognizes the basic distinctions between Israel and the church.[12] However, there are other changes in the relationship between God and humanity that are not acknowledged by everyone. In addition, there are two more major features of dispensationalism that serve to distinguish it from other theological approaches.

A Second Major Aspect of Dispensationalism

A second major aspect of dispensationalism is the insistence that the nation of Israel must be held "distinct" from the church.[13] Some today speak of the church as the *New Israel*. Yet even a superficial reading of the Bible reveals that many of the commands and promises that were given to the nation of Israel are distinct from the commands and promises given to the church. This is not to say that there is not some degree of overlap between the two peoples of God or the relationship between them.[14] However, an important implication of this distinction is that God's program and purposes for Israel have not been abandoned, but rather await complete fulfillment in history. Non-dispensationalists, on the other hand, tend to either deny any future in history for the nation of Israel or spiritualize and merge God's promises to Israel with his promises to the church.[15]

This important distinction between Israel and the church is based upon the first fundamental principle of dispensationalism already discussed: Scripture should be interpreted in a literal manner. Again, though many non-dispensationalists would affirm this interpretive approach in theory, in practice they fail to employ it in a *consistent* manner. As a consequence, they tend to reinterpret the Old Testament in light of New Testament revelation. Dispensationalists, on the other hand, insist that the Old Testament must be interpreted in its original context and upon its own terms. Only after properly understanding the Old Testament in this straightforward way can we then seek to integrate or fit together its teachings with later teachings provided by the New Testament.[16] At the end of the day, the result of the dispensational approach is to see two distinct plans and purposes for Israel and the church in history. This truth will be made clearer in succeeding chapters.

A Third Major Aspect of Dispensationalism

Ultimately, as some of the definitions cited previously suggest, the purpose of each dispensation is to fulfill the plan and purposes of God and bring glory to Him (cf. Eph. 1:3–14, 3:10). This is the third defining characteristic of dispensationalism. That is, a major emphasis of dispensationalism is the *doxological* (from the Greek noun *doxa*, meaning *glory*) purpose of Biblical history. While other systems of theology may speak of God's glory, only dispensationalism comprehensively applies this thought to the entirety of human history and beyond. Thus, the purpose of God in human history is not simply to redeem people from the consequences of their sin, as important as that may be. His larger purpose in all that He does is to bring glory to Himself. As Ryrie puts it: "The differing dispensations reveal the glory of God as He manifests His character in the differing stewardships, which culminate in history with the millennial glory."[17] Sadly, sometimes that is accomplished by God's righteous judgment of human rebellion.

The result of this emphasis is an understanding of human history in which God is glorified *within* history through events that take place on this present Earth rather than outside of the history of this Earth in the eternal state, when there will be "a new heaven and a new earth" (Rev. 21:1). In this manner, human sin and evil, which were introduced during the first dispensation (innocence), will be utterly vanquished during the final dispensation (kingdom). Stated another way, what went awry in the garden of Eden because of the sin of the first Adam will be rectified, or set straight, in the promised future kingdom on Earth (also known as the millennium) because of the rule of the last Adam, Jesus Christ (cf. Rom. 5:12–21).

This view of the course of human history is more logically satisfying and ultimately more glorifying to God than non-dispensational systems of thought. In those approaches, history is viewed as a continual struggle between good and evil that is abruptly ended by the sudden termination of this present world and the corresponding inauguration of the eternal state.[18] Unfortunately, this type of victory over sin and evil has no relationship to events upon the Earth. Such a scenario is comparable to a football game being decided not by one of the teams achieving victory on the field of play but rather by the owner of the stadium arbitrarily declaring an end to the game. More satisfying is the dispensational approach in which Jesus scores the winning touchdown.

Some Additional Characteristics of a Dispensation

Besides the definition of a dispensation, it is also important to understand certain common characteristics of a dispensation. One prominent characteristic is that, in each dispensation, a specific *responsibility* is given by God to humanity. Accordingly, one leading dispensationalist defines dispensationalism as, "An approach to the Bible that recognizes differing responsibilities for people, in keeping with how much they knew about God and His ways."[19] In most dispensations, these responsibilities are clearly spelled out in the form of specific revelation, which is often given by God to mankind at the beginning of that dispensation.

For example, within the *dispensation of law*, God's expectations for the nation of Israel are clearly spelled out in the commandments and ordinances that comprise the Mosaic Law (Exodus, Leviticus, Numbers and Deuteronomy). However, in other instances, the responsibilities given to humanity by God must be inferred from the Scriptural texts that correspond to a particular dispensation. The *dispensation of conscience*, for example, contains no clearly defined requirements or responsibilities for the family of Adam and succeeding generations. Rather these expectations must be inferred from the various, relatively brief episodes in Genesis 4 to 8 that comprise this dispensation.

Some dispensationalists have sought to distinguish a responsibility from what they call a *test* for humanity in each dispensation. But, as Ryrie points out: "The test is practically the same as the human responsibility. . . . In one sense every dispensation contains the same test: Will a person respond favorably toward the responsibility of the particular economy [or dispensation] under which he is living?"[20]

Corresponding to the responsibility or test given to humanity in each dispensation is the overall *failure* on the part of humanity to fulfill that responsibility.[21] That is, each dispensation is characterized by an overall failure of humanity as a whole to fulfill the assigned responsibilities. Of course, there are often notable exceptions, such as the family of Noah during the *dispensation of conscience* or Daniel the prophet during the *dispensation of law*, who distinguished himself as a man of God in the midst of the spiritual failure of the nation as a whole.

In addition, the failure of humanity to meet God's expectations in a given dispensation is climaxed in the form of a *judgment* from God that signals the end of one dispensation and the beginning of the next one. For example, as we will see, the *dispensation of conscience* ends with the world full of violence and the corresponding judgment of the worldwide flood of Noah upon all of humankind (Genesis 6–8).

Similarly, the *dispensation of kingdom* will end with humanity's rebellion at Satan's instigation against King Jesus and God's corresponding judgment upon those who rebel (Rev. 20:7–9). A chart illustrating the responsibilities and judgments that correspond to each dispensation can be found at the conclusion of this chapter.

Summary of the Dispensational Scheme

In summary, we can say that dispensationalism is the story of how God has tested the will and character of people in virtually every conceivable manner possible. Yet, each time they have utterly failed the test. Unfortunately, as will be seen in the chapters ahead, ensuing generations have largely disregarded these historic tests and failures, even to this day. However, on the positive side, dispensationalism is also the story of God's mercy and grace toward humanity despite its rebellion and failure. Each time mankind fails, we see God again and again providing a means of redemption and hope for the future. These facts will be abundantly illustrated in the upcoming chapters.

When looked at in another way, dispensationalism is a theological *system* or a way of organizing the data of Scripture into logical categories. As in any system of organizing data, certain repeated patterns and primary truths come to the forefront. In the case of dispensationalism, these patterns and truths become the distinguishing features of the system and, as such, provide theological signposts that guide the student of Scripture in the proper interpretation of a particular passage.

For example, virtually all dispensationalists affirm a pretribula-tional rapture of the church, which is the belief that Jesus will catch up to heaven his church, both the living and dead, prior to a seven-year period of great tribulation and judgment upon the earth (Matt. 24:4–31; 1 Cor. 15:51–52, 1 Thess. 4:13–18). However, the *timing* of the rapture as pretribulational is not an explicit teaching of the New Testament, though Revelation 3:10 is a strong candidate for such a teaching.[22] Rather, belief in a pretribulational rapture is primarily an inference drawn from the data of Scripture on the basis of the prin-ciples of dispensationalism.[23] Appendix 1 provides a brief defense of the pretribulational rapture.

Finally, we should note that dispensationalism presently exists in two major forms known as *classical* or *traditional* dispensationalism and an additional form known as *progressive* dispensationalism. While the differences between the two systems of theology are worthy of discussion and debate, for the most part they both affirm the same scheme of human history as presented in this volume. Appendix 2 provides a brief overview and critique of progressive dispensationalism from a classical dispensational perspective.

Discussion Questions

1. What is meant by the term *literal interpretation*? How might this concept be misunderstood?

2. How does dispensationalism differ in its interpretive

approach to the Bible from other systems of theology?

3. What is meant by the term dispensationalism?

4. What is a dispensation?

5. What is the second major feature of dispensationalism?

6. Why do dispensationalists insist that the Old Testament be interpreted in its original context upon its own terms, before seeking to integrate its teachings with later teachings provided by the New Testament? What can occur if this does not happen?

7. What is the third major feature of dispensationalism?

8. What are two primary characteristics of each dispensation?

9. Why does dispensationalism offer a more satisfying and God-glorifying perspective of history?

THE SEVEN DISPENSATIONS

	Innocence	Conscience	Government	Promise	Law	Grace	Kingdom
Scripture	Genesis 1–3	Genesis 4–8	Genesis 9–11	Genesis 12–Exodus 18	Exodus 19–Acts 1	Acts 2–Revelation 19	Revelation 20
Duration	From the creation of Adam to his fall	From the fall of Adam to the flood of Noah	From the flood to the call of Abraham	From the call of Abraham to the giving of the Mosaic Law	From the giving of the Mosaic Law to Pentecost	From Pentecost to the second coming of Christ	From the second coming to the new heaven and new earth
The Responsibility before God	Fill and steward the earth; do not eat from the tree	Obey the dictates of conscience	Replenish the earth; rule righteously	Live in light of the promise	Keep the covenant (Mosaic)	Believe the gospel and make disciples	Worship and obey Christ, the King
The Judgment from God	Separation from God	The flood	Confusion of language	Egyptian slavery	The curses of the covenant and the captivities	The judgment seat of Christ and the great tribulation	Fire from heaven

CHAPTER 1:

LIFE IN PARADISE

The Dispensation of Innocence (Gen. 1–3)

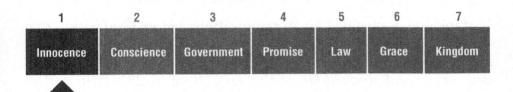

1	2	3	4	5	6	7
Innocence	Conscience	Government	Promise	Law	Grace	Kingdom

nyone who has ever been around small children knows that modesty is not one of their concerns. Depending upon the circumstances, little children can be prone to streaking around the house in their birthday suits. According to Genesis 2:25, the first man and the first woman (Adam and Eve) were initially both naked and were not ashamed by their nakedness. You could say they were in a state of *innocence*, somewhat like two-year-olds who run around naked and think nothing of it.

For this reason, the first dispensation is called *innocence*.[24] While the word *innocence* is not found in Genesis 1 to 3, this dispensation refers to that initial period of human history when humanity existed in a non-sinful state as created by God. According to Genesis 1:31, everything God created "*was* good" in the beginning (Gen. 1:4, 10, 12, 18, 21, 25, 31). That is, God created all things without any taint of sin or corrupting influence. Consequently, Adam and Eve were sinless people, who felt no sense of guilt or shame, nor did they need to at this point. Their physical nakedness was symbolic of their moral and spiritual innocence.[25]

Obviously, people do not run around naked anymore. So what changed? Recall that each dispensation is characterized by a unique arrangement, or relationship, between God and humanity that includes a specific human responsibility before God within that relationship. The responsibilities given to our first parents included *procreation* and *stewardship* of the earth (Gen. 1:28). That is, they were commanded by God to produce children and then to assume the responsibility of stewarding or caring for God's creation. Within this general stewardship responsibility, they were tasked with the cultivation of the garden of Eden (Gen. 2:15).

In addition to these general responsibilities, Adam and Eve were given individual responsibilities. According to Genesis 1:26–28, both the man and the woman were created "in the image of God" (Gen. 1:27). Therefore, both shared equally in the attributes that have been conferred upon humanity. Likewise, men and women today have equal standing before God in Christ (cf. Gal.

3:28). However, contrary to much popular thinking today, this does not mean there are no differences between the sexes. In fact, the differences between men and women are intended by God so that a husband and his wife will complement one another in marriage. When God created Eve, He said she was intended to be "a helper comparable to him" (Gen. 2:18). Literally, this phrase can be translated as "a helper corresponding to him."

Now, the term *helper* sounds somewhat demeaning to our modern ears. But most times in the Bible, the same term is actually used to describe God. For example, in Psalm 33:20 we read:

> Our soul waits for the LORD;
> He *is* our help and our shield.

So, in fact, the term *helper* and the role it implies carries with it a sense of dignity and honor. The idea of "a helper corresponding to him" then suggests that the woman is both his equal as well as one who supplies that which he needs or lacks. As God's provision, she *complements* or completes him.[26]

The fact that God created the man first suggests something that other texts of Scripture confirm: God gave to the man the responsibility to lead his family as the head of the household. Correspondingly, the wife is called by God to graciously submit to the loving leadership of her husband (see Eph. 5:22–31; 1 Pet. 3:1–7). The Scriptures exhort "husbands . . . to love their own wives as their own bodies" and "as Christ also loved the church," His bride

(Eph. 5:28, 25). So it is that kind of love to which the Lord exhorts a wife's submission.

Unfortunately, because of sin, today the differences in the roles and responsibilities of husbands and wives often lead to conflict. This will be clearly seen when we deal with the next dispensation. Even today, by and large, men have failed to provide the kind of leadership in their marriages and families that God intends for them to provide. Instead, they have either abused their authority as head of the home, or they have abdicated it altogether.

It is in this critical role of providing loving leadership to his wife that Adam utterly failed. According to Genesis 2:17, our first parents were forbidden to eat "of the tree of the knowledge of good and evil." Even though it is popularly believed that tree was an apple tree, the Bible does not indicate what kind of fruit the tree bore. But that detail is not important. Rather, what is important is that this prohibition was designed as a test of whether or not Adam and Eve would freely choose to obey God because, as of yet, their *innocence* had not been tested. But that was about to change.

As seen in Genesis 3:1–7, the devil disguised himself as a serpent and "deceived" (Gen. 3:13; 1 Tim. 2:14) Eve into partaking of the forbidden fruit (vv. 2–6a). She then gave it to her husband to eat as well (v. 6b). Notice that Adam was "with her" (Gen. 3:6). That is, he likely was standing right next to her, listening to the conversation between the serpent and Eve. And yet, incredibly, he never spoke up. He never interrupted the conversation to warn Eve of the consequences of what she was being tempted to do.

He was, in a word, *passive*. But what a price they both would pay for his passivity!

As already mentioned, each dispensation is characterized by *failure*. Accordingly, this first dispensation ended with the failure to fully fulfill the responsibilities given to Adam and Eve by God. Through blatant disobedience, Adam and Eve disobeyed the only prohibition God gave them. In fact, we are informed by Paul that Adam ate from the forbidden tree with a conscious understanding that he was rebelling against God (1 Tim. 2:14).

The consequences of that rebellion and disobedience were catastrophic and correspond to the *judgment* that ends this dispensation. Adam's sin is what theologians often refer to as *the fall*. The first consequence of this fall was that sin and death entered the world for the first time. As the Apostle Paul observes: "Through one man sin entered the world, and death through sin, and thus death spread to all men" (Rom. 5:12). Notice that immediately after Adam and Eve sinned against God, the Bible says: "Then the eyes of both of them were opened, and they knew that they *were* naked; and they sewed fig leaves together and made themselves coverings" (Gen. 3:7). In other words, their innocence was gone. They now knew firsthand what good and evil were all about.

Also, God had warned Adam and Eve that once they disobeyed Him they would "surely die" (Gen. 2:17). However, they did not die physically, at least not right away. In fact, the Bible says that Adam lived to the ripe old age of 930 years (Gen. 5:5). So did God fail to fulfill his warning? Not at all. What happened was that Adam and

Eve experienced *spiritual separation from God.* Death according to the Bible is the experience of a separation. When a person dies physically the body is separated from the spirit or the immaterial aspect of their being (Js. 2:26). When a person dies spiritually, they are separated from God, which is the state of every human being born into this world (Eph. 2:1–3). As Paul tells his Gentiles readers: "Remember . . . that at that time you were without Christ . . . having no hope and without God in the world" (Eph. 2:11–12). In the case of Adam and Eve, this spiritual separation was symbolically represented by their physical expulsion from the Garden of Eden and from the presence of God that they had previously enjoyed (Gen. 3:24).

Another consequence of our first parents' sin was that God's wonderful creation fell under a curse (Gen. 3:17–18). The earth was affected in such a way that the process of harvesting its fruit became extremely difficult, frustrating and unfulfilling. As Paul observes, "The creation was subjected to futility. . . . The whole creation groans and labors with birth pangs together until now" (Rom. 8:20, 22). Further effects of this curse include a host of natural disasters that God never intended for humanity to experience, such as hurricanes, tornadoes, droughts, pestilences and earthquakes. Ironically, humanity—created to be the ruler over all creation (cf. Gen. 1:26–28)—has now become, in some sense, subservient to the created realm. As we will see in our study of the dispensation of government, mankind's relationship with nature was aggravated even further following Noah's flood (cf. Gen. 9:2).

Interestingly, many today contend that people are born into this world in a state of innocence or with a morally blank slate. Subsequently, they are corrupted by their environment. But in this dispensation of innocence we see that even in a perfect and sinless environment, people utterly failed to obey God. Yet, in the midst of their failure, God gave Adam and Eve—and all of their posterity— hope that He would one day provide a special "Seed" that would crush the power of the serpent (Gen. 3:15). Most Bible scholars refer to this promise by the Latin term *protoevangelium*, which means "first gospel." In other words, this is the first promise of a future Redeemer who would save humanity from the condemnation of their sin. Of course, we know today that this promise was fulfilled thousands of years later in the Person of Jesus Christ.

Meanwhile, God temporarily provided for the guilt of Adam and Eve by taking away their fig-leaved loincloths and replaced them with loincloths made of animal skins (Gen. 3:21). This death or sacrifice of an animal established a principle and pattern that was repeated throughout the Old Testament. That is, the forgiveness of human sin must be secured through the death of an innocent substitute in order to satisfy the justice of God. As the author of Hebrews puts it: "Without shedding of blood there is no remission" (Heb. 9:22). Ultimately, it was the sacrifice of Jesus, called "the Lamb of God" (John 1:29), that secured the basis of the potential forgiveness and salvation of all humanity (1 John 2:2; 4:14). Of course, receiving that forgiveness and salvation is conditioned upon faith in Jesus (Rom. 3:23–25).

At this point, someone might object: "Wait a minute! Adam and Eve sinned, not me. Why am I suffering for their mistake? That's not fair!" While that is a naturally expected response, the answer to the objection is that in the providence and wisdom of God, *Adam perfectly represented us.* His decisions and actions represented the entire human race (see Rom. 5:12–21). As a result, we are all born into this world spiritually separated from God. In fact, the Bible says that prior to faith in Christ we are *enemies* of God. That is, we are naturally predisposed to rebelling against and disobeying God.

But there is good news: God loves his enemies! As the Apostle Paul writes:

> But God demonstrates His own love toward us, in that while we were still sinners, Christ died for us. . . . For if when we were enemies we were reconciled to God through the death of His Son, much more, having been reconciled, we shall be saved by His life. (Rom. 5:8, 10)

Was it "fair" that one man, and a wholly innocent man at that, suffered for all of mankind? No, it was not fair. In fact, it was the height of injustice. But Christ's death on our behalf was also the most amazing demonstration of God's love and grace. So you have to decide what you want: fairness or grace?

Discussion Questions

1. Why is this first dispensation referred to as innocence?

2. What were the responsibilities that God gave to humanity in this dispensation?

3. In what way did Adam and Eve fail to fulfill those responsibilities?

4. What were the judicial consequences of this failure?

5. How did God provide hope for Adam and Eve and their posterity?

6. What is the significance of God's clothing of Adam and Eve with animal skins?

7. What would you say to someone who charged God with being unfair by imputing Adam's sin and guilt to all of humanity?

CHAPTER 2:

DOING THINGS MY WAY

The Dispensation of Conscience (Gen. 4–8)

1	2	3	4	5	6	7
Innocence	Conscience	Government	Promise	Law	Grace	Kingdom

D o you normally refer to yourself or introduce yourself to others as a sinner? Probably not. And if we are totally honest, we probably do not like the designation sinner very much either. Yet, the Bible is clear that every human being is born into this world as a sinner (cf. Ps. 51:5; Eph. 2:1–3). As we saw in the previous chapter, after the fall Adam and Eve became sinners, and the effects of their sinful nature began to show themselves very quickly.

Following their expulsion from the Garden of Eden, Adam and Eve had many children (Gen. 5:4). Two of them were Cain and

Abel (Gen. 4:1–2).[27] We must read between the lines, but apparently God began to require regular offerings or sacrifices to Himself (Gen. 4:3–5). On one particular occasion, both Cain and Abel brought an offering, and while God was pleased with Abel's offering, He was displeased with Cain's. Now we are not told why God was displeased with Cain's offering. Some say it was because he did not bring a blood sacrifice (cf. Heb. 9:22). However, since we are not told the reason for the offerings, this is at best conjecture. Also, in the Mosaic Law certain non-bloody offerings were acceptable to God.

The real reason for God's displeasure with Cain's offering seems to be the *heart* with which Cain presented his offering. As the Bible clearly teaches elsewhere, God is not interested in offerings and sacrifices that are mere outward formalities. (See, for example, Isaiah 1:1–17 and Matthew 5:23–24.) Rather, His primary concern is with the heart of the worshiper. As Jesus Himself said about certain Jews of his time:

> These people draw near to Me with their mouth,
> And honor Me with *their* lips,
> But their heart is far from Me. (Matt. 15:8)

Interestingly, Cain's occupation as "a tiller of the ground" (Gen. 4:2) aligned him more with the recently cursed earth (Gen. 3:17), while Abel's occupation as "a keeper of sheep" was more in tune with God's original mandate to exercise "dominion over ... the earth" (Gen. 1:28). This does not mean God likes you more if you milk cows than if you grow corn. But these brief descriptions hint at some deeper heart attitudes that become more evident in the worship of God offered by the two brothers.[28]

In addition, while the description of Cain's offering is quite ordinary, the description of Abel's offering indicates that he went out of his way to please God. That is, he offered "the firstborn of his flock and of their fat" (v. 4). In other words, Abel offered to God his best. Accordingly, we are told that "the LORD respected," "had regard for" (NASB), or "looked with favor on" (NIV), "Abel and his offering." Millennia later, the author of Hebrews commends Abel for his faith by which he received "witness" from God "that he was righteous" (Heb. 11:4).

In response to God's rejection of his offering, "Cain was very angry" (Gen. 4:5). However, there is no question regarding whether or not he understood God's expectations because he never takes issue with God's unhappiness with his offering. Then, in response to Cain's "angry" reaction, God appeals to Cain's *conscience* in this matter by giving him another opportunity to do the right thing but also warning him of the consequences of yielding to his sinful "desire" (Gen. 4:6–7). As one commentator puts it: "When Cain practices what is right, there will be an uplifted face, meaning a good conscience before God without shame."[29]

For this reason, dispensationalists refer to this stage of human history as the dispensation of conscience. At this point in human history there is no indication that God had given any *written* laws to Adam and his posterity. And so, as seen in God's interaction with Cain, people's relationship with God seems to have been governed by God on the basis of their conscience. Thus, the responsibility given to mankind in this dispensation is to live righteously before God on the basis of a God-given conscience.

Thousands of years later the Apostle Paul wrote:

> For when Gentiles, who do not have the law, by nature do the things in the law, these, although not having the law, are a law to themselves, who show the work of the law written in their hearts, their conscience also bearing witness, and between themselves *their* thoughts accusing or else excusing *them*. (Rom. 2:14–15)

Even today, people seem to intuitively agree about what is right and what is wrong, which is evidence of the conscience that God has placed in every human heart from the very beginning of human history.

Unfortunately, Cain refused God's overtures to be properly reconciled to God. This refusal then led to Cain's murder of his brother, Abel (v. 8). Once again God confronts Cain about his sin, but this time he pronounces judgment upon Cain (vv. 10–12). Cain does not dispute the fact of his sin, though initially he tries to deny his knowledge of it (v. 9). Apparently, he already knew that what he had done was sinful because he acknowledges that God's pronouncement of a curse upon him is, in fact, a "punishment" (v. 13).

In response, Cain self-centeredly complains that his punishment is disproportionate to his crime because he now believes his life will be in danger (vv. 13–14). Apparently, Cain did not feel his murder merited his own death. In fact, we see no evidence of remorse on Cain's part for what he did. Interestingly, in response to Cain's complaint, God graciously forbids his execution and puts a mark on him to warn people from taking matters into their own hands (v. 15). Clearly, God is claiming for himself, and rightly so, the sole prerogative of taking a life. At least at this point in human history, capital punishment was not an option, but this would soon change.

Cain's subsequent journey "from the presence of the LORD" (Gen. 4:16) echoes the expulsion of Adam and Eve "from the presence of the LORD God" (Gen. 3:8) and accentuates the deepening depravity in Cain's life and in the human race. In fact, Lamech, a direct descendent of Cain, boasts to his two wives—the first recorded departure from God's design for marriage—of a double murder he committed (vv. 23–24; see NASB). Ironically, he expresses his acts of violence through the medium of a poem. This is a poignant reminder that as fallen creatures created in the image of God, we are capable of such great beauty as well as such great savagery. Accordingly, in Genesis 6 we see that Cain's act of violence comes to characterize the whole earth (vv. 5, 11–13). Apparently, God's mercy to Cain only served to multiply evil, rather than restrain it.

Some today believe that through sufficiently proper education, people will do what is right. Because we are all *basically good*, having a *spark of divinity*, all we truly need is for someone to point us in the right direction and we will go there. Yet, as the story of Cain and his posterity clearly illustrates, and even as the daily news confirms continuously, knowing the right course of action does not necessarily result in following through with it. Although Cain knew God's expectations, he chose to defy them. The problem with the human mind and heart is not a lack of *information* but rather an abundance of *contamination*: People are born with a depraved heart, and as a result, they corrupt every relationship and every action (cf. Rom. 1:28–32; 2:14–24). Over time their consciences become "seared" (1 Tim. 4:2), with the effect that they heartily approve of inherently sinful conduct (Rom. 1:32). In fact, one day, the conscience will become the basis of God's judgment (Rom. 2:15–16). Only the regenerative power of the Holy Spirit on the basis of Christ's shed blood can "cleanse your conscience" sufficiently in order to enable you "to serve the living God" obediently (Heb. 9:14; cf. 10:22).

In God's initial appeal to Cain, he warned Cain that if he refused to do what is right, he would open himself up to the ravages of sin, which are like a "crouching" animal of prey, ready to devour him (Gen. 4:7, ESV). Unfortunately, Cain did not heed the warning, and the first recorded human born into this world became a murderer. Here we see the first salvo fired in the battle between the ungodly *seed of the serpent* and the godly *Seed of the woman* that the Lord had prophesied in Genesis 3.

As already noted, in Cain's succeeding generations, we see a steady downward spiral morally. But besides the increase in violence, there are other indicators. Though God had condemned Cain to wander the earth (Gen. 4:12), Cain defied the Lord once again by settling in the land of Nod and then building a city. And instead of honoring God, Cain chooses to honor his son by naming the city after him (Gen. 4:17). Banished from God's presence, people decide to fill their lives with pursuit of the things of this earth (Gen. 4:20–22). They are very inventive—like their Creator. But there is not one mention of the Lord in all of this inventiveness. Like many today, they decided to enjoy the creation apart from the Creator.

On the heels of this great failure of humanity to live righteously before God on the basis of their conscience, this dispensation ends with the cataclysmic judgment of the flood of Noah (Gen. 7–8). At this point in time,

> Then the LORD saw that the wickedness of man *was* great in the earth, and *that* every intent of the thoughts of his heart *was* only evil continually. (Gen. 6:5)

Clearly, mankind utterly failed the test to live in an obedient manner before God on the basis of his conscience.

However, once again God provides hope through the line of another son of Adam, Seth (Gen. 4:25–26). Eventually, one of Seth's descendants, Noah, finds "grace in the sight of the Lord" (Gen. 6:8). This is the first use of the word "grace" or "favor" (ESV) in the Scriptures.[30] Through Noah and his family, God once more provides hope for the future, and this hope results in the commencement of the next dispensation.

Discussion Questions

1. Why is this dispensation named the dispensation of conscience?

2. What is the evidence of humanity's sin following the fall of mankind?

3. What is the evidence of God's mercy toward mankind despite their rebellion?

4. In what ways is the experience of the time prior to the flood being repeated today?

5. What lessons can we learn from humanity's inability to live rightly on the basis of conscience alone?

6. How does the experience of Enoch (Gen. 5:21–24) provide additional evidence of God's mercies during this dispensation? See also Hebrews 11:5–6.

Some today believe that through sufficiently proper education, people will do what is right. Because we are all basically good, *having a* spark of divinity, *all we truly need is for someone to point us in the right direction and we will go there. Yet, as the story of Cain and his posterity clearly illustrates, and even as the daily news confirms continuously, knowing the right course of action does not necessarily result in following through with it. Although Cain knew God's expectations, he chose to defy them. The problem with the human mind and heart is not a lack of* information *but rather an abundance of* contamination!

1	2	3	4	5	6	7
Innocence	Conscience	Government	Promise	Law	Grace	Kingdom

ave you ever had a project you were working on go wrong—really wrong? What did you do? You probably had three options: try to fix the problem, start all over again from scratch or give up. As we have seen in the first two dispensations, there was a project that God was working on called the human race, and it went really wrong. In fact, things were so bad that God expressed sorrow or grief that He even created mankind in the first place (Gen. 6:6–7). This does not mean that God did not anticipate what happened. Rather, this is a common figure of speech in the Bible to help us as human beings comprehend God's response to human sin and, in this case, it is used to underscore the utter depravity of the human race.[31]

So what did God do? Well, as you may already know, God decided to start over. God sent a flood that wiped out all of mankind except for Noah and his family. You may ask, "Why just one man and his family? Why did God not save hundreds or thousands of people?" That is a good question. We may also ask, however, why did God create a world in which He knew before He created it that the vast majority of humanity would reject Him? Honestly, the Bible does not directly answer these questions. Instead, the Word of God emphasizes two truths that help us at least partially understand God's mind on this matter.

First, the Bible teaches very clearly that God desires all people to be saved. As the Apostle Peter puts it:

> The Lord is not slack concerning *His* promise, as some count slackness, but is longsuffering toward us, not willing that any should perish but that all should come to repentance. (2 Pet. 3:9)

Similarly, the Apostle Paul affirms: "God our Savior . . . desires all men to be saved and to come to the knowledge of the truth" (1 Tim. 2:3-4). According to Genesis 6:3, despite the utter depravity of humanity, God patiently waited 120 years while Noah built the ark. We are also told by the Apostle Peter that, during this time, Noah "preached to the" people who ultimately perished in the flood (1 Pet.

3:19–20; 2 Pet. 2:5). Clearly, God gave that generation ample opportunity to turn from their sinful ways and to trust in Him, which is consistent with His desire that all would be saved. Tragically, no one responded to Noah's preaching with repentance and faith. Therefore, only his wife, his three sons and their wives were spared (Gen. 7:7).

The second truth we need to understand is that God desires that people *freely* choose him.[32] God could have made a world in which everyone automatically loved Him from the very start. But could we really call that *love* in the truest sense of the word? Can you imagine a world in which your spouse, your children, your family and your friends loved you only because they took a special pill every day? Would that kind of love be something that would thrill your heart?

We could wish that people everywhere would use their power to choose by loving and serving God. But the reality is they do not. The reality, according to Jesus, is that the majority choose the road to destruction and that there are few that choose the path to eternal life (Matt. 7:13-14). After three years of ministry, performing many miracles, preaching and teaching the very people who were about to crucify him, Jesus said:

> O Jerusalem, Jerusalem, the one who kills the prophets and stones those who are sent to her! How often I wanted to gather your children together, as a hen gathers her chicks under *her* wings, but you were not willing! (Matt. 23:37)

Clearly, Jesus lays the blame for the refusal to come to him in faith at the feet of those who make such a choice. Likewise, the blame for the destruction of virtually all of humanity during the flood of Noah must be laid at the feet of the very people who chose to disregard the preaching of Noah.

Following the flood, God restated to Noah and his family the command He originally gave to Adam and Eve: They were told, "Be fruitful and multiply, and fill the earth" (Gen. 9:1; cf. 1:28). Thus, this original responsibility given to humanity is still in effect, and nowhere in the remainder of the Bible do we find it rescinded. While spouses have greater freedom today to determine how many children they will have, the consequences of resisting this mandate are generally seen on a national level, where nations which have birthrates that are below two are finding it difficult to maintain a growing economy.[33]

God also informed Noah (and all his posterity) of two important changes in the aftermath of the previous dispensation. First, he tells them that they may now eat animal meat (Gen. 9:3). Apparently, ever since the creation of Adam and Eve, people had been vegetarians (cf. Gen. 1:29). Now, as Genesis 9:2 suggests, a new antagonism began to exist between humans and animals that would complicate humanity's responsibility to "subdue . . . and rule over" the animal kingdom (Gen. 1:28, NASB). So God now gives people permission to use animals for food. Likewise, Paul, in response to a heresy that forbade the eating of certain foods, wrote: "For every creature of God *is* good, and nothing is to be refused if it is received with thanksgiving" (1 Tim. 4:4). The one caveat God adds is that such meat should not be eaten with blood (Gen. 9:4). As verse 5 implies, blood is equated with life.

By forbidding the eating of blood, this restriction implicitly instills a respect for the sacredness of all life.

Such respect for the sacredness of all life is continued in a second and more significant change. Specifically, the Lord declares that anyone who takes another human's life shall forfeit his own (Gen. 9:5–6). The reason God gives for this injunction is that:

> . . . in the image of God
> He made man. (Gen. 9:6)

That is, the innate sanctity of human life is invoked as the basis for this ultimate punishment, known today as capital punishment. Of course, many today reject the use of capital punishment as an essentially barbaric act, unworthy of the dignity of civilized society. However, when correctly understood and employed, capital punishment actually affirms human dignity. As the late Christian apologist C. S. Lewis puts it: "To be punished, however, severely, because we deserved it . . . is to be treated as a human person made in God's image."[34]

Recall that following Cain's murder of his brother Abel, God spared Cain's life and even threatened severe consequences upon anyone who might try to kill him. After the great loss of life in the flood, succeeding generations might think that God has little regard for human life and that taking a life is a small matter. Because of this, God directs that from that point on, taking a human life would merit capital punishment. God does not specify the logistics of *how* capital punishment was to be carried out, except to say that human beings collectively ("by man") will be the agents of that punishment. However, most agree that this is human government in seed form. In support of this, Paul specifies in Romans 13:4 that human government "is God's minister" and as such has been empowered with the authority to conduct capital punishment.[35] Subsequently, in his defense before Festus, Paul said: "If I am an offender, or have committed anything deserving of death, I do not object to dying" (Acts 25:11). Here Paul acknowledges that there are deeds "deserving of death."

For this reason, this third dispensation is called the *dispensation of government*. It should be obvious that this dispensation was instituted in response to the utterly violent chaos that reigned from Cain's day until the flood. The utter failure of mankind during the dispensation of conscience showed the need for law and order. This need defines the primary purpose of government to restrain evil. The Apostle Paul confirms this purpose when he says that "rulers are" to be "a terror" or deterrent to bad behavior (Rom. 13:3). He then states that government is "God's minister to you for good . . . an avenger to *execute* wrath on him who practices evil" (v. 4). Similarly, Peter states:

> Therefore submit yourselves to every ordinance of man for the Lord's sake, whether to the king as supreme, or to governors, as to those who are sent by him for the punishment of evildoers and *for the* praise of those who do good. (1 Pet. 2:13–14)

Again, we see human government is authorized to act in God's stead.[36]

Now perhaps some may wonder how this authority God supposedly has given to human governments squares with the sixth commandment: "Thou shalt not kill" (Ex. 20:13; KJV). The answer is that the Hebrew word translated "kill" in the King James Version of this commandment most often refers to either the act of murder or causing another's death through negligence, otherwise known as involuntary manslaughter. Therefore, most modern versions translate the sixth commandment in this manner: "You shall not murder" (NKJV, NASB, ESV, NIV). In addition, this Hebrew verb is never used to refer to killing that takes place in war. Thus, there is no conflict between the mandate of Genesis 9:6 and succeeding revelation by God. Rather, as Paul makes clear in Romans 13, God has delegated to human government the authority to exercise capital punishment in the case of murder.[37]

Unfortunately, despite the fresh beginning, we see the ugly reality of the same old human sin all too soon. Surprisingly, it appears first in the life of righteous Noah. No sooner does Noah conclude one of the greatest physical, emotional and spiritual feats in human history than he gets drunk (Gen. 9:21). There is also a related moral failure on the part of his son Ham that leads Noah to prophesy about the moral failings of his descendants—beginning with his son, Canaan—the progenitor of the Canaanites, who became one of the most sinful and perverse nations on the planet at that time (Gen. 9:25).[38]

Not surprisingly, this dispensation also ends in failure at the Tower of Babel (Gen. 11). There humanity sought to defy God's mandate to "fill the earth" (Gen. 1:28) by joining together through one common language in order to "make a name for" themselves and "build . . . a tower whose top *is* in the heavens" (Gen. 11:4). In a sense, they were trying to fulfill a God-given desire in a sinful manner. God created man in his own image, and as such, He gave him a responsibility with a Divine sense of purpose and significance. As a result, we know intuitively in our hearts that we are so much more than the sum of the molecules in our bodies. Along with that knowledge, we have an inner desire to be someone, to achieve something of significance. In a few words, we were created for greatness. But how do we achieve that greatness? There are only two ways: either through obedience to God or in rebellion against Him.

Regrettably, this generation of people sought to achieve greatness in rebellion against God in order to make their mark and be remembered forever. Their sin lay not so much in the act of building a city and a tower as it was in using these things as a means of prideful self-exaltation. In response, God judges them by confounding and multiplying their languages and scattering "them ... over the face of all the earth" (v. 8; cf. vv. 7–9). However, when viewed from another perspective, this judgment was also an act of mercy. By confounding mankind's ability to communicate effectively and by scattering them into smaller ethnic groups, their potential for evil was considerably diminished (v. 6).

Interestingly, many today believe that humanity's answer to its problems lies in a one-world government. In fact, one day the world will achieve, at least momentarily, what this Genesis generation sought; they will be united religiously through a one-world religious system that will be wholly opposed to Christ and His followers (cf.

Rev. 17:1–6), and they will be united politically in their allegiance and worship of the future Antichrist (cf. Rev. 13:3–8). The world will finally achieve its goal of unified self-worship. But at what cost? Tragically, most of that future generation will suffer the eternal judgment that is reserved for Satan (cf. Rev. 13:8; 14:9–11; cf. 19:19–21).

Many today also believe that mankind's problems can be solved politically or through a certain form of government (e.g., communism). However, human history has amply demonstrated that governments, if functioning properly, can only restrain evil. They are not especially effective agents for promoting good. Also, when governments are excessively restrictive of the basic rights of human beings, progress— in every sense of the word—is severely impaired.

However, because God ordained government, it should be viewed as fundamentally a good institution. Some Christians oppose service in government because of their view that it is an inherently corrupt institution. But they have no firm Biblical grounds for this position. Godly Joseph and Daniel both served within secular governments for pagan rulers. In fact, the Scriptures make it clear that God was the one who orchestrated their positions of service (cf. Gen. 50:5–7, 20; Dan. 1:9, 17–21, 6:1–3, 28). At the same time, however, their experience was sometimes a difficult one to say the least.

One final note before we conclude this chapter: as should already be obvious, even though we are no longer living in the dispensation of government, the changes instituted by God at the beginning of that dispensation are still in effect today. In fact, certain aspects of previous dispensations are sometimes carried over to succeeding dispensations.

For example, God not only continues to relate to mankind in general through human government (cf. Rom. 13:1–7), He also continues to do so on the basis of conscience (cf. Rom. 2:15). Of course, we are dependent upon the progress of revelation to discern correctly what former responsibilities may still be in effect and which may have been eliminated.

Discussion Questions

1. Why did God decide to start over with the human race?

2. In what ways did the world change after the flood?

3. How do society's views on capital punishment compare with the Biblical view?

4. Why should government be viewed as something for our good?

5. Why do you suppose God is so opposed to one-world government?

6. According to the Bible, what should be the Christian's response when governments abuse their authority? (See Acts 4:18–19 and 5:29.)

7. What are some of the challenges—as well as opportunities—a Christian would face if serving in a governmental role?

"

Interestingly, many today believe that humanity's answer to its problems lies in a one-world government. In fact, one day the world will achieve, at least momentarily, what this Genesis generation sought; they will be united religiously through a one-world religious system that will be wholly opposed to Christ and His followers (cf. Rev. 17:1–6), and they will be united politically in their allegiance and worship of the future Antichrist (cf. Rev. 13:3–8). The world will finally achieve its goal of unified self-worship. But at what cost? Tragically, most of that future generation will suffer the eternal judgment that is reserved for Satan (cf. Rev. 13:8; 14:9–11; cf. 19:19–21).

"

CHAPTER 4:

LOOKING FOR A FEW ... FAITHFUL MEN

The Dispensation of Promise (Gen. 12–Ex. 18)

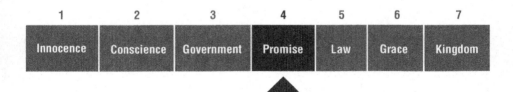

1	2	3	4	5	6	7
Innocence	Conscience	Government	Promise	Law	Grace	Kingdom

Who in our world today—or in your life—would you consider to be a person of faith? What is it about their life that demonstrates their faith? The next dispensation begins with such a person who is known for his faith. In fact, he is revered in three of the world's major religions: Judaism, Christianity and Islam. His name, as you might have already guessed, is Abraham.

The failure of humanity to obey God on the basis of human government led to a new dispensation in which God focused upon building a righteous nation from one man, Abraham. According to the Scriptural record, Abraham was called by God while living in the city of Ur in the Mesopotamian Valley in the southeast region of the modern nation of Iraq (Gen. 15:7).[39] "Not knowing where" God was calling him (Heb.11:8; cf. Gen. 12:1), he left his country by faith and was led by God to the land of Canaan.[40]

This new dispensation, which extends from God's call of Abraham to the Exodus of Israel from Egypt, is called the *dispensation of promise*.[41] It takes its name from the fact that God made a number of magnificent promises to Abraham, his son Isaac and his grandson Jacob, otherwise known as the patriarchs. As the author of Hebrews states regarding Abraham: "By faith he dwelt in the land of promise as *in* a foreign country, dwelling in tents with Isaac and Jacob, the heirs with him of the same promise" (Heb. 11:9; cf. 6:15). These promises also constitute the first of the Biblical covenants, commonly referred to as the Abrahamic Covenant. The Abrahamic Covenant is initially pronounced by God in Genesis 12:1–3. It is also reiterated and elaborated upon God throughout the book of Genesis (i.e., 13:14–17, 15:5–18, 17:1–22, 22:16–18). This covenant provides the basis for understanding God's purposes for both the future nation of Israel as well as all mankind. It is also the foundation for all succeeding covenants God made with the nation of Israel, which will be discussed in detail in coming chapters.

Within the Abrahamic Covenant, Abraham and his posterity are promised three things. First, God promises him a land for an everlasting possession (Gen. 17:8; cf. 12:1, 7; 13:14–15, 17; 15:18,

22:17–18; 26:4; 28:13; 48:4). This land, of course, is what is commonly referred to today as the land of Israel. However, the boundaries God gave to Abraham extend far beyond the national boundaries of Israel, both historically and in modern times (cf. Gen. 15:18–21).[42]

God's second promise to Abraham was numerous offspring "as the stars of the heaven and as the sand which *is* on the seashore" (Gen. 22:17; cf. 12:2; 13:16; 15:5; 17:14–17; 26:4; 28:14; Heb. 11:12). Initially, Abraham is promised "a great nation" (12:2). Later that promise is expanded to "nations," and Abraham is also told, "Kings shall come from you" (17:6).

The third promise God gives to Abraham is that he and his posterity will have the privilege of being God's instrument of blessing for all nations (Gen. 12:3; 18:18; 22:18; 26:4; 28:14). Interestingly, Paul quotes this promise and says that through it God "preached the gospel to Abraham beforehand" (Gal. 3:8). In this manner Paul says, the nations are blessed through the greatest descendant of Abraham, Jesus Christ, when they put their faith in Jesus and receive the blessing of justification by faith.

It is important to note that the provisions of this covenant were initially fulfilled in a *literal* fashion: Abraham's descendants literally inherited the land of promise under Joshua. And numerous offspring, as well as kings and nations, literally descended from Abraham. This strongly implies that God intends to bring to complete and literal fulfillment *all* that He has promised. It also strongly implies that the fulfillment of future covenants, based upon the Abrahamic Covenant, will also take place in a literal fashion.

As we have observed already, this hermeneutical, or interpretive, approach to Scripture is a primary emphasis of dispensationalism in contrast to other approaches which employ a non-literal hermeneutic when dealing with Old Testament covenantal promises and prophecies concerning the nation of Israel.

Interestingly, neither Abraham, his son Isaac nor his grandson Jacob personally experienced the fulfilment of these promises. Instead, they "dwelt" as nomads "in the land of promise" (Heb. 11:9). However, as the author of Hebrews states, they were enabled to see the fulfillment of these promises "afar off" (Heb. 11:13).[43]

The story of the sojourn of Abraham, Isaac and Jacob in the land of promise is a fascinating one, as they lived by faith as "strangers and pilgrims" (Heb. 11:13) "in the land of promise" (Heb. 11:9), and this story is filled with many relevant lessons for us today as we also seek to trust God "as sojourners and pilgrims" upon this earth (1 Pet. 2:11; cf. 1:1, 17). Unfortunately, as with other dispensations, this dispensation also ends with the failure of mankind to fulfill the responsibilities God gave to him. Abraham, Isaac and especially Esau and Jacob, as well as his great-grandsons, demonstrated multiple lapses of faith and obedience, which increased in severity as time went on. In fact, the last 400 years of this dispensation find the descendants of Abraham, now the 12 tribes of the nation of Israel, in bondage in Egypt (cf. Gen. 26:2–3). Thus, mankind's ability to live righteously in his own world, even with the blessing of God, fails miserably by the third generation.

But once again, God graciously intervened to reverse the fortunes of Israel and all mankind.

First, in one the greatest stories of Divine vindication in the Bible, God sovereignly worked through the sinful motivations of Jacob's sons to send their brother, Joseph, into Egypt in order to prepare the way for the entire family to survive a terrible seven-year famine. Then, after 400 years of terribly repressive bondage in that country, God raised up a deliverer—Moses—who led his people out of Egypt in a journey to the land promised to Abraham, Isaac and Jacob (Ex. 3:16–17).

In the history of Western civilization, there are many examples of those who advocated that the way to build a just world was to get away from the rest of the world and start fresh with a community of people dedicated to the same righteous purposes (e.g., the Pilgrims). The problem with this endeavor, however, was that after just a few generations those purposes were either compromised or forgotten altogether.

Thus, this fourth dispensation serves as a preview of those failures and a lesson to humanity today that only through the regenerating and sanctifying work of the Spirit of Christ in the hearts and lives of those who have placed personal faith in Christ can people be changed in such a manner as to effect the kind of lasting changes that truly please God. However, before that reality is realized, there is one more dispensation that tests the capacity of human beings to live righteously before God in their own strength. That is the subject of the next chapter.

Discussion Questions

1. From where does the dispensation of promise get its name?

2. What are the major stipulations of the Abrahamic Covenant?

3. What evidence is there that God will fulfill the terms of this covenant in the future?

4. What specific example of the lapses of faith and obedience of Abraham, Isaac, Jacob and their families can you recall from Genesis 12 to 50?

5. In what ways does the story of Joseph and his brothers (Genesis 37 to 50) parallel the experience of Jesus? Note: Many students of the Bible regard Joseph to be what is known as a *type* of Christ or an Old Testament foreshadowing of a New Treatment reality.

6. What personal encouragement can you draw from God's dealings with the patriarchs?

In the history of Western civilization, there are many examples of those who advocated that the way to build a just world was to get away from the rest of the world and start fresh with a community of people dedicated to the same righteous purposes (e.g., the Pilgrims). The problem with this endeavor, however, was that after just a few generations those purposes were either compromised or forgotten altogether.

CHAPTER 5:

CAN WE FOLLOW INSTRUCTIONS?

The Dispensation of Law (Ex. 19–Acts 1)

1	2	3	4	5	6	7
Innocence	Conscience	Government	Promise	Law	Grace	Kingdom

H ave you ever been singled out for special attention? Maybe it was a special opportunity to display your talents or gifts. Maybe it was "the luck of the draw." Or maybe it was the call of God upon your life. In this next dispensation, we see God singling out the nation of Israel for special attention in ways that no other nation before or since has ever been singled out.

As briefly mentioned at the conclusion of the last chapter, under the leadership of Moses, God delivered the nation of Israel from bondage in Egypt through a mighty demonstration of his power over the false gods of Egypt, including Pharaoh himself (Ex. 12–14). Then, at the foot of Mount Sinai the Lord made a proposal to the people through Moses (19:4–6). There, God offered to make the nation of Israel "a special treasure to Me above all people" (v. 5). In other words, of all the nations upon the earth, Israel was to become the object of special attention from the God of the universe. They would also have the responsibility of representing God to the nations as "a kingdom of priests and a holy nation" (v. 6). This amazing proposition represented a key step in the fulfillment of God's promises to Abraham, Isaac and Jacob, otherwise known as the Abrahamic Covenant, given 400 years earlier.

However, in this proposed plan, God refers to another covenant (v. 5), a new covenant, which is commonly referred to as the Mosaic Covenant. There are a couple of important aspects of this covenant that should be borne in mind. First, the Mosaic covenant was offered to a *redeemed* people. As God states to Israel in v. 4: "I bore you on eagles' wings and brought you to Myself." In other words, their redemption from slavery in Egypt was wholly due to the gracious work of God on their behalf. In the same way, every true believer in Jesus is redeemed from the guilt and condemnation of their sin by the gracious work of God on their behalf (Eph. 2:8–9). However, identifying Israel as a redeemed people does not mean that every person in the nation was in a saving relationship with the Lord. Rather, the nation as a whole was being viewed as in a right relationship with God.

Second, because the Mosaic Covenant was made with a redeemed people, its purpose was not to effect the salvation of that people. As Paul explained to the Christians in Galatia: "By the works of the law [contained in the Mosaic Covenant] no flesh shall be justified" (Gal. 2:16; cf. Acts 13:39). And to the Christians at Rome he declared: "Therefore by the deeds of the law no flesh will be justified in His sight, for by the law *is* the knowledge of sin" (Rom. 3:20; cf. Ps. 143:2). Indeed, Paul says one of the purposes of the law of Moses was to increase transgressions or to give to sin the character of transgression so that people might be even more conscious of their sinfulness and their corresponding need of salvation from sin (Gal. 3:19; cf. Rom. 4:15, 7:9–11).[44]

So what was God's primary purpose in giving Israel the law? The purpose of the law was to *regulate* the relationship between God and his people. This was accomplished through 613 commandments, or laws, contained in the books of Exodus, Leviticus, Numbers and Deuteronomy, which governed every aspect of the life of the Israelites. For example, there were *moral* laws, such as the ten commandments. There were *civil* laws, such as rules for properly doing business within the nation and conducting judicial trials. And there were *ceremonial* laws, such as those that instructed the Israelites in how to offer appropriate sacrifices to the Lord. Since the phrase *the law* (or what Jews refer to as the Torah) is often used in the Bible to refer to this extensive body of commandments and ordinances, this dispensation is called the *dispensation of law.*

Obviously, the responsibility given to humanity, and specifically to Israel, in this dispensation was to obey the law. In fact, the Lord promised great material and social blessing in exchange for obedience to the law: Their numbers would multiply abundantly, their fields and animals would be fruitful, and their enemies would be at peace with them (Deut. 28:1–14; Ps. 81:10–16). Even before Israel had formally received the law from the hand of Moses, God promised them:

> If you diligently heed the voice of the LORD your God and do what is right in His sight, give ear to His commandments and keep all His statutes, I will put none of the diseases on you which I have brought on the Egyptians. For I *am* the LORD who heals you. (Ex. 15:26)

This unprecedented promise of blessing in exchange for obedience uniquely characterizes this dispensation. Never before nor since has God made such blanket promises of physical and societal health in exchange for obedience to him. Conversely, if they disobeyed God, they would suffer *curses* that would result in the loss of their blessing and prosperity. Disease, famine and subjugation to their enemies were some of the penalties they would incur (Deut. 28:15–35). In addition, on an individual basis, disobedience to the law was often met with strict penalties, including death in cases of the most severe disobedience. So while there was the promise of great blessing in keeping the law there was also the warning of severe discipline for transgressing it.

The people of Israel, perhaps somewhat presumptuously, readily agreed to the Lord's proposition: "All that the LORD has spoken we will do" (Ex. 19:8; cf. 24:3). However, even before Moses had finished receiving the law from God, the Israelites disobeyed God in a heinous act of idolatry and immorality (Ex. 32:1–6). And despite a severe punishment of the nation at that time (Ex. 32:25–35), with few exceptional periods, this type of behavior continued to characterize the next 700 years of Israel's history.

Finally, God followed through on his warning and the nation was carried away into exile in two phases: The 10 northern tribes were carried away by the Assyrians in 722 B.C., and the two southern tribes were carried away by the Babylonians, beginning in 605 B.C.—the first of three deportations by King Nebuchadnezzar that ended with the destruction of the temple and the walls of the city of Jerusalem in 586 B.C. (2 Kings 24:1–25:21; cf. Dan. 1:1–4). Though a remnant of approximately 50,000 Jews eventually returned to the land of Israel 70 years later in accord with the prophecy of Jeremiah (Jer. 25:11–12; cf. Dan. 9:1–2), from that time on the nation and its people were subjected to Gentile domination through a succession of world empires (cf. Dan. 7–8).

Some people say, "Just tell me what you want me to do and I'll do it." In fact, many believe that our society's problems can be remedied with more education, under the assumption that if people understand right from wrong they will by nature choose to do the right thing. Yet, history has amply demonstrated the opposite. Even with the promise and the frequent experience of abundant blessing and miraculous provision from the hand of the Lord, Israel failed miserably and repeatedly to obey God's law (cf. Rom. 10:21).

Yet, despite their disobedience, God in his grace and mercy continued to affirm His promise that was given to Moses and the people in the desert of Sinai to make Israel the chief of the nations. Throughout Israel's history, God promised to provide a specially anointed king, the Messiah, who would establish His kingdom on earth and rule both his people and the entire world from Jerusalem (Joel 3:9–21; Amos 9:11–15; Isa. 2:1–4, 9:6–7, 11:1–16, 26:6–9). Significantly, this promise continued to be affirmed even after the nation's severe judgement of exile (Jer. 31:27–38, 33:1–13; Dan. 7:13–14, 9:24–27; Mic. 4:1–8; Zeph. 3:14–20; Zech. 8:1–8, 14:9–21).

That promise began to be fulfilled with the birth of Jesus (cf. Luke 1:31–33). Accordingly, when Jesus began his public ministry, he made a *bona fide* offer of this promised kingdom to the people of Israel. However, this offer was made contingent upon their repentance (Matt. 3:2; 4:17; Mark 1:14). Unfortunately, the nation as a whole and its leadership refused to do this. Instead, they crucified their Savior. This represented the ultimate failure of the nation of Israel and brought to conclusion this dispensation. Though some of God's promises made repeatedly through the prophets still remain to be fulfilled, Israel has been temporarily set aside in the plan of God (see Rom. 11).

Of course, God had anticipated, and even foreordained, Israel's rejection of her Messiah (Acts 2:23), and He used this event to provide salvation for all peoples through the death of Jesus on the cross in order that He might create a new entity, the church (Matt. 16:18, Acts 1:4–8). As God had done throughout Israel's history, He preserved a faithful remnant within the nation (cf. Isa. 1:9), and these believing Jews became the nucleus of the early church (Acts 2:1–4, 41–47; cf. Rom. 9:29, 11:1–6).

The good news is that the means of salvation today are no longer restricted to one nation or to one place but are available to "everyone who calls on the name of the Lord" (Rom. 10:13, ESV). Interestingly, the Apostle Paul says the law was intended to function as a "tutor *to lead*" the Jews to an understanding of their need for a Savior (Gal. 3:24, NASB). Unfortunately, the nation in the time of Jesus and his disciples failed to understand their need. As the Apostle Paul explains in his letter to the Christians in Rome, "They being ignorant of God's righteousness, and seeking to establish their own righteousness, have not submitted to the righteousness of God" (Rom. 10:3). That is, being ignorant of the righteous and holy character of God, they sought to save themselves through their own good works, rather than receive the only means of salvation and true righteousness through Jesus Christ (Rom. 3:22–26). Even today, most Jews remain blind to their need for a Savior (Rom. 11:25)—along with the vast majority of the world's population, who are ignorant of their sinful and hopeless state before a holy God (2 Cor. 4:3–4; Eph. 2:11–12, 4:17–19).

The good news, however, is that one day the nation of Israel will turn again to the Lord (Rom. 11:25–27; cf. Heb. 8:8–12), and the Lord will fulfill the promises to Israel that He made long ago through the prophets (Rom. 11:28–29). Paradoxically, this great national revival will take place during the darkest and most terrifying period in human history, known commonly as the *tribulation* (Matt. 24:21, 29). But before we discuss this event further, we need to understand the present dispensation of grace, which is the focus of the next chapter.

Discussion Questions

1. Discuss the proposal that God made to Israel through Moses. What were its benefits and what were its responsibilities?

2. What was the primary purpose of the law? What was it not intended to do?

3. In what ways did Israel fail in her responsibilities during this dispensation? How did God respond to Israel's failures?

4. How did God reassure the nation of Israel of the certainty of his promises to them?

5. Why do you suppose the nation of Israel rejected Jesus' offer of the prophesied kingdom?

6. How did God use Israel's failure to provide salvation for the entire world?

7. What do the Scriptures promise with regard to the future of the nation of Israel?

8. In what ways do God's dealings with the nation of Israel encourage you?

The purpose of the law was to regulate the relationship between God and his people. This was accomplished through 613 commandments, or laws, contained in the books of Exodus, Leviticus, Numbers and Deuteronomy, which governed every aspect of the life of the Israelites.

CHAPTER 6:

EVERYTHING IS ON THE HOUSE

The Dispensation of Grace (Acts 2–Rev. 19)

1	2	3	4	5	6	7
Innocence	Conscience	Government	Promise	Law	Grace	Kingdom

W hat would you say is the most important question you have ever answered? When you were a child or young person, the most important question may have been: "What would you like to do when you grow up?" As a young adult, the most important question may have been: "Will you take this person to be your lawfully wedded spouse?" Or perhaps it was: "Will you take this job offer?"

As important as the answers to these questions may be, they pale in comparison to what the Bible teaches is the most important question you can answer: "Who is Jesus?" Why is that the most important question people should answer? Because the answer you provide to that question will determine not only the quality of your life here on earth now but also where you will spend the rest of eternity. As Peter confessed to Jesus:

> Lord, to whom shall we go? You have the words of eternal life. Also we have come to believe and know that You are the Christ, the Son of the living God. (John 6:68–69)

In our postmodern age, this way of thinking may seem arrogant and intolerant, but according to the Scriptures it is no more arrogant than insisting that two plus two equals four. Because once you understand who Jesus really is, you discover that He is one of a kind. There are no legitimate competitors. For this reason, the dispensation under consideration in this chapter is not only unique but exceptionally so, because it encapsulates the life God offers through faith in Jesus. And in human history there has never been a better offer.

Following Christ's death, resurrection and ascension into heaven, the dispensation of grace was inaugurated with the coming of the Holy Spirit upon 120 disciples of Jesus who were gathered in an upper room (Acts 1:12–15, 2:1–4). The title *dispensation of grace* can be misleading because it suggests that God had not been gracious before. In fact, Ryrie admits that dispensationalists could do a better job of highlighting God's demonstrations of grace in prior dispensations.[45] However, compared to previous dispensations, God's grace is *so much more evident* in this dispensation that even the Scriptures use this terminology to draw a contrast with the previous dispensation of law.

As the Apostle John puts it: "For the law was given through Moses, *but* grace and truth came through Jesus Christ" (John 1:17). The law represents God's standard of righteousness, a standard that no one, save Jesus Christ, has been able to achieve. But God in his grace imparts the righteousness that He demands through the law when sinners trust in Jesus for their salvation. As a result, God no longer views them as sinners but as the saints that they have become in Christ. That is truly grace!

Another illustration of the gracious nature of this dispensation is seen just a few verses earlier, where John summarizes the incarnation of Jesus in this way: "And the Word became flesh and dwelt among us, and we beheld His glory, the glory as of the only begotten of the Father, full of grace and truth" (John 1:14). In other words, the full extent of God's glory is revealed in Jesus, because He is the ultimate expression of God's "grace and truth." There was and is no greater expression of God's grace than in the giving of "His only begotten Son" for the sins of the world (John 3:16). Likewise, the Apostle Paul speaks of the grace of God as personified in the person of Jesus Christ, when he writes: "For the grace of God that brings salvation has appeared to all men" (Tit. 2:11).

As suggested earlier, part of the gracious nature of this present dispensation is that every true believer in Jesus Christ now has

God Himself living within them through the Holy Spirit. In fact, so prominent is the Person of the Spirit in this dispensation that we could call this the *dispensation of the Holy Spirit*. The Apostle John anticipates this when he recounts an episode in the ministry of Jesus, during one of the feasts of the Jews:

> On the last day, that great *day* of the feast, Jesus stood and cried out, saying, "If anyone thirsts, let him come to Me and drink. He who believes in Me, as the Scripture has said, out of his heart will flow rivers of living water." (John 7:37–38)

Then John explains what Jesus was referring to:

> But this He spoke concerning the Spirit, whom those believing in Him would receive; for the Holy Spirit was not yet *given*, because Jesus was not yet glorified. (John 7:39)

Here we see that John draws a distinction between the days in which Jesus lived on earth and a future time following Jesus' resurrection and ascension into heaven. As a matter of fact, before ascending to heaven, Jesus told his disciples to remain in Jerusalem "for the Promise of the Father," because "you shall be baptized with the Holy Spirit not many days from now" (Acts 1:4–5). This promise was fulfilled on the day of Pentecost with the vivid coming of the Holy Spirit upon the early disciples, being accompanied by "a sound . . . as of a rushing mighty wind" and "tongues, as of fire" (Acts 2:2-3). The apostles also spoke in "tongues" or other languages on that first Pentecost day as a visible sign of the Spirit's arrival to the many Jewish pilgrims gathered in Jerusalem on that occasion (Acts 2:14–18; cf. 1 Cor. 14:22).

The implication of this very significant event in Acts 2, as prophesied by Jesus in John 7:39, is that prior to this time God's people did not enjoy the privilege of the indwelling Holy Spirit in this way. That is, even though there were times in which "the Spirit of God came upon" certain persons, such as prophets or kings, for the performance of some service to God (Num. 24:2; cf. Judg. 15:14; 1 Sam. 10:10, 19:20), the people of God in general did not enjoy the regular indwelling ministry of the Holy Spirit enjoyed by Christians today.

One of the many benefits of this indwelling presence of the Holy Spirit is that believers are no longer required to obey an *external* law with no *internal* means of help (cf. Rom. 7:8–12, 14; 8:3). Rather, through the Holy Spirit, believers are empowered to obey God from the heart (John 14:16–17, 26; 16:12–15; Gal. 2:20, 5:16–25). For this reason, Paul can say Christians "are not under law but under grace" (Rom. 6:14; cf. 7:6). That is, the law of Moses no longer functions today as the means by which God governs His relationship with His people. Rather, Christians are led by the Holy Spirit as the Spirit applies the truths of God's Word to their lives (cf. Rom. 8:14, Gal. 5:16–18).

This does not mean, however, that Christians are without any moral or spiritual guidelines. What it means is that, on the one hand, they are freed from the burden of seeking to please God through numerous laws that regulate every aspect of their lives (Gal. 5:1, 13; cf. Acts 15:10, 28–29). On the other hand, it means they are empowered to obey God's will from the heart, sometimes referred to as "the law of Christ" (Gal. 6:2; cf. 1 Cor. 9:21, ESV ; cf. Matt. 11:28–30). As Paul puts it, God's grace through Jesus is "teaching us" to be obedient to the Lord (Tit. 2:12).

By the way, these wonderful blessings and provisions are a direct result of the New Covenant, which God originally promised to Israel (see Jer. 31:31–34; cf. Ezek. 36:25–27). Through the shedding of His blood on the cross, Jesus inaugurated the New Covenant (Matt. 26:27–28; Luke 22:20; cf. 1 Cor. 11:15; 2 Cor. 3:6; Heb. 9:15). As the bride of Christ, the church partakes in some of the blessings promised in the New Covenant, which are discussed above. However, the complete fulfillment of the New Covenant promises will not occur until Christ returns one day to reign upon the Earth (Rom. 11:26–27).[46]

Another distinguishing feature of this dispensation is the union of Jews and Gentiles "in one body" (Eph. 2:16; cf. vv. 11–22). That Gentiles were to be saved in large numbers someday was not a new revelation. Many passages in the Old Testament, and especially the book of Isaiah, herald a coming day of worldwide Gentile salvation (Isa. 42:6b–7; 49:6b–7; cf. Ps. 98:3). But the fact "that the Gentiles should be fellow heirs, of the same body" (Eph. 3:6) was a new revelation. The Apostle Paul refers to his new revelation as "the mystery of Christ . . . which in other ages was not made known to the sons of men" (Eph. 3:4-5). This marks a significant distinction from the previous dispensation.

One more aspect of this dispensation that needs to be highlighted is the major responsibility that has been given to the church, otherwise known as the great commission. As Jesus declares in Matthew 28:19–20, the church has been commissioned to "go into all the world" (Mk. 16:15) "and make disciples" (Matt. 28:19). Thus, whereas the nation of Israel failed to represent God to the nations, the church has now been called to do the same. In fact, Peter appropriates the same language that is used by God with Moses in His invitation to Israel in Exodus 19:5–6 and says to his fellow Christians:

> But you *are* a chosen generation, a royal priesthood, a holy nation, His own special people, that you may proclaim the praises of Him who called you out of darkness into His marvelous light. (1 Pet. 2:9)

This does not mean that the church has taken on the *identity* of Israel, but she has taken on the *role* of Israel in relation to the world.

Unfortunately, despite the wonderful and abundant spiritual provisions of God through Christ that have been given to people to live righteously before Him (i.e., Eph. 1:3–13; 3:14–20), this dispensation will also end in failure. According to the Apostle Paul, in the last days of this dispensation many who profess an allegiance to Christ will turn away from Him, both doctrinally and morally (2 Tim. 3:1–5, 13; 4:3–4). Also, the world as a whole will reject Christ (Ps. 2:1–3; cf. Rev. 19:19). Instead they will embrace a false Christ, known commonly as "the Antichrist" (1 John 2:18, 4:3; cf. Rev. 13).

But prior to the most horrifying seven years this world has ever seen, God in his grace will rapture His church off the earth (1 Cor. 15:51–52;

1 Thess. 4:13–18; Rev. 3:10). Even during this tribulation period, God will graciously send forth his Word through a specially chosen group of 144,000 Jewish believers in Jesus, and as a result, many who were left behind on earth will turn to the Lord (Matt. 24:14; Rev. 7). However, as already noted, by and large the world will reject the message of these Jewish evangelists to believe the lies given to them by the Antichrist.

This dispensation will finally conclude with a great battle (often referred to as the battle of Armageddon; see Rev. 16:12–15; 19:17–21), in which the forces of evil will be destroyed and Jesus will return to earth with his previously raptured bride, the church, to establish the kingdom that God promised long ago through the Old Testament prophets to Israel (Rev. 19:11–20:6). The details concerning this kingdom are the subject of the next chapter and the final dispensation.

Discussion Questions

1. Why is this dispensation referred to as the *dispensation of grace*?

2. Describe the ministry of the Holy Spirit in this present dispensation. How does it differ from His ministry during the *dispensation of law*?

3. What is the relationship between Jews and Gentiles in this dispensation (Eph. 2:11–3:6)?

4. What responsibility, previously held by Israel, is the church called to fulfill?

5. How will this dispensation end? What applications can you draw for your own life from this sobering prediction?

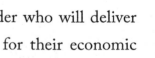

1	2	3	4	5	6	7
Innocence	Conscience	Government	Promise	Law	Grace	Kingdom

How much our world longs for a leader who will deliver them from their fears and provide for their economic needs. And how often has a politician or other world leader promised to do this and yet failed time after time. In this final dispensation, the *perfect world leader* will finally arrive. Yet, as we shall see once again, even under His rule the world will rebel.

After six dispensations, each of which ended in mankind's failure to obey God, God will give humanity one final chance to vindicate itself through the seventh dispensation, the *dispensation of kingdom*. In this dispensation, Jesus Christ will return to earth to establish his long-prophesied and awaited kingdom and will rule over the entire world (Dan. 7:13–14; Zech. 14:9; Matt. 25:31–46; Rev. 19:15). In fact, there will be two phases to the Lord's kingdom. The first is frequently referred to as the millennium, since according to Rev. 20:4–6 it will last 1,000 years.[47] This comprises the dispensation of the kingdom. The second phase of the kingdom will follow the creation of "a new heaven and a new earth" (Rev. 21:1; cf. Isa. 65:17). This will be the eternal state itself.

To properly understand the basis for this dispensation, we need to understand one more covenant that God made with the nation of Israel, known as the *Davidic Covenant* (Ps. 89:3–4). In 2 Samuel 7:8–16, in response to David's request to "build a house for" the Lord (2 Sam. 7:5), God makes several promises:

- He "made (David) a great name" (vv. 8–9; cf. Gen. 12:2).

- He will grant Israel a permanently secure "place of their own" (vv. 10–11a; cf. Gen. 13:15, 17:8).

- He "will establish his kingdom" from a direct descendent of David (vv. 11b–13; cf. Jer. 33:15, 17).

- God's relationship with this descendent will be as a father to a son (v. 14).

- God will never revoke these kingdom promises (v. 15; cf. Ps. 89:30–35; Jer. 33:20–21)

- "I will establish the throne of his kingdom forever" (vv. 13b, 16; cf. Ps. 89:28–29, 36–37)

In hindsight, we can see that some of these promises were fulfilled in the life of David's son, Solomon. However, it is only in Jesus Christ that complete fulfillment will be realized. As the angel Gabriel announced to Mary, the mother of Jesus:

> He will be great, and will be called the Son of the Highest; and the Lord God will give Him the throne of His father David. And He will reign over the house of Jacob forever, and of His kingdom there will be no end. (Luke 1:32–33; cf. vv. 68–69)

This announcement was, in fact, anticipated hundreds of years earlier through the prophet Isaiah, who declared:

> For unto us a Child is born,
> Unto us a Son is given;
> And the government will be upon His shoulder.
> And His name will be called
> Wonderful, Counselor, Mighty God,
> Everlasting Father, Prince of Peace.
> Of the increase of *His* government and peace
> *There will be* no end,
> Upon the throne of David and over His kingdom,
> To order it and establish it with judgment and justice
> From that time forward, even forever.
> The zeal of the LORD of hosts will perform this. (Isa. 9:6–7; cf. Jer. 33:14–18; Luke 2:29–32; Acts 3:19–21)

So what will it be like to live during the millennium? Well, in a word it will be a near-paradise. Christ will rule and reign with perfect "righteousness" (Isa. 9:7, ESV; cf. Isa. 11:1–5, 42:1–4; cf. Ps. 96–99). His resurrected saints will "rule" and reign with him (Rev. 2:26–27, 3:21, 20:4–6 cf. 1 Cor. 6:2). Satan's influence will be muted, as he will be "bound" during this time (Rev. 20:2) and unable to influence events upon earth as he now does (2 Cor. 4:4; Eph. 6:12; 1 Pet. 5:8, 1 John 5:19). And war and civil strife will be abolished (Isa. 2:1–4; 11:9–10; 65:17–25; 66:10–14; Zech. 14:11).

In addition, conditions upon earth will be restored to a status that is similar to what Adam and Eve enjoyed before their disobedience (Matt. 19:28; Rom. 8:20–23; cf. Isa. 65:17, 66:22). For example, the earth will yield great productivity (Joel 2:21–26; Amos 9:13); human life will again experience great longevity (Isa. 65:20); natural and social evils will be abolished (Isa. 29:18–20; Zeph. 3:19); and animals will become vegetarian again (Isa. 11:6–9, 65:20; cf. Gen. 1:30).

Unfortunately, there will be one critical, negative aspect to this dispensation: The people who will populate this first phase of the Lord's eternal kingdom will still need to be saved from sin. This is due to the fact that the initial inhabitants are those who have survived the seven–year tribulation period and will be ushered into the Lord's kingdom at the commencement of the millennium (Matt. 25:31–34). Having not yet died, they will still possess their sinful and mortal bodies. In that state, some of them will give birth to children, who will likewise have sinful and mortal bodies no different from children today.

And because of their sinful condition, some will chafe under the rule of Christ, and those who refuse to submit to him will experience God's judgment (Zech. 14:16–19; cf. Ps. 2:8–12).

Incredibly, despite the righteous rule of Christ and the enjoyment of paradise–like conditions, this dispensation will also end in mankind's failure to honor God as they should and submit to the righteous rule of King Jesus, which will be the fundamental responsibility given to humanity during this dispensation. According to Revelation 20:7–9, Satan will be set loose upon the earth again for a short season, and he will succeed in inciting the majority of earth's inhabitants to attack Jerusalem, the city from which Christ will reign during the millennium (Zech. 14:16–17). But the Lord will send fire from heaven to crush the rebellion, and Satan will be finally "cast into the lake of fire . . . forever and ever" (Rev. 20:10). The final judgment of all the wicked dead of all the ages, sometimes referred to as the "great white throne" judgment (Rev. 20:11–15), will take place at this time. They too will be cast into the lake of fire since, tragically, their names will be absent from the all–important "*Book* of Life" (Rev. 20:12, 15)—the roll of those who have trusted in Christ for their salvation (Phil. 4:3, cf. Rev. 3:5).

After God puts down this final rebellion, He will create "a new heaven and a new earth" (Rev. 21:1). Upon this *new earth* there will rest the New Jerusalem, in which "there shall be no more death, nor sorrow, nor crying. There shall be no more pain" (Rev. 21:4; cf. vv. 2, 27). The redeemed of all the dispensations will enjoy intimate fellowship with God (Rev. 21:3, 7). "And they shall reign forever and ever" (Rev. 22:5).

Discussion Questions

1. Explain the two phases of the future kingdom. In what ways will they differ?

2. How does the Davidic Covenant provide a basis for the future millennial kingdom?

3. Describe some of the features of the millennial kingdom. Which are the most significant in your mind and why?

4. What major responsibility will people have toward God in this dispensation? How will their failure to fulfill that responsibility be dealt with?

5. How will this dispensation end? How does this final dispensation provide a convincing proof of humanity's utter depravity before God?

The people who will populate this first phase of the Lord's eternal kingdom will still need to be saved from sin. This is due to the fact that the initial inhabitants are those who have survived the seven-year tribulation period and will be ushered into the Lord's kingdom at the commencement of the millennium (Matt. 25:31–34). Having not yet died, they will still possess their sinful and mortal bodies. In that state, some of them will give birth to children, who will likewise have sinful and mortal bodies no different from children today.

CHAPTER 8

WAIT A MINUTE!

Objections to Dispensationalism

N̲ot surprisingly, there are several objections to the dispensational system of understanding Scripture that we have just described. However, while a few may have had some validity at one time, today none of these objections stands up to closer scrutiny.

First, the charge is made by some non-dispensationalists that dispensationalism is a relative newcomer to the theological scene and, therefore, does not merit serious consideration. For example, Millard J. Erickson, the author of a popular systematic theology that is influential among evangelicals, insists that there is "no trace of this theology"[48] in the church fathers.

However, the most important question to answer for any proffered system of understanding Scripture is not how old a viewpoint is, but whether or not it accurately reflects the teaching of Scripture. Actually, dispensationalism first appeared in an incipient form more than 300 years ago in the writings of the French philosopher Pierre Poiret (1646–1719), who "developed a scheme of seven dispensations covering the scope of Scriptures and history."[49] Subsequently, others presented "dispensational" schemes, including John Edwards (1639–1716) and Isaac Watts (1674–1748).[50]

However, John N. Darby (1800–1882), an Anglo-Irish Plymouth Brethren pastor, is considered by most to be the "Father of Dispensationalism" as we know it today. Beginning about 1827, Darby began to disseminate widely the truths that formed the core of later dispensationalism, including "the absolute separation of Israel and the Church into two distinct peoples of God, and the separation of the Rapture (the 'catching away' of the Church) from Christ's Second Coming."[51] Then in the 1870s, Darby came to America and, during a series of preaching tours, he won over a number of influential evangelical church leaders to the dispensational system he taught, including William E. Blackstone, James H. Brookes, James M. Gray and C. I. Scofield.[52]

Subsequent to Darby, dispensationalism was greatly popularized in the 20th century by men such as Scofield (editor of the influential *Scofield Reference Bible*[53]), Lewis Sperry Chafer (founder and first president of Dallas Theological Seminary), Alva J. McClain (former president of Grace Theological Seminary), Charles C. Ryrie (former DTS professor and editor of *The Ryrie Study Bible*[54]), John F. Walvoord (former DTS professor and its second president) and J. Dwight Pentecost (former DTS professor). Thus, despite determined opposition from non-dispensational quarters, dispensational thinking has passed the test of time and, over several centuries, has enjoyed the support of numerous scholars who are committed to the literal approach to Biblical interpretation as described in the introduction.

Another frequent objection to dispensationalism is that it teaches more than one way of salvation. However, it must be insisted that—despite some unfortunate remarks by Scofield and Chafer many years ago that seem to imply that there has been more than one way of salvation[55] —dispensationalists today universally affirm that salvation has always been by grace through faith in every dispensation. As Ryrie explains:

> The basis of salvation in every age is the death of Christ; the *requirement* for salvation in every age is faith; the *object* of faith in every age is God; [however] the *content* of faith changes in the various dispensations.[56]

Curiously, some non-dispensationalists teach that Christ was the conscious object of faith for every saint of every age. For example, in his three-volume systematic theology, Charles Hodge (1797–1878) asserts:

> It was not mere faith or trust in God or simple piety, which was required, but *faith in the promised Redeemer* or faith in the promise of redemption through the Messiah. . . . the Church has been one and the same under all dispensations. It has always had

the same promise, the same Redeemer, and the same condition of membership, namely, *faith in the Son of God as the Saviour of the world.*[57]

However, Ryrie rightly points out that "it is very difficult, if not impossible, to prove that the *average* Israelite [for example] understood the grace of God in Christ."[58] As one non-dispensationalist admits: "That, to satisfy God, God must die, that men might inherit God, to be with God, was *incomprehensible* under the Old Testament seminal knowledge of the Trinity, the incarnation, and the crucifixion followed by the resurrection."[59] Indeed, even Jesus' own disciples did not comprehend His need to die—even after His crucifixion (Luke 24:25–26; cf. Matt. 16:21–23; Luke 9:43–45).

A third frequently voiced criticism of dispensationalism is that dispensationalists see no contemporary use for large swaths of the Scriptures, including some portions of the New Testament itself. Admittedly, in the history of dispensationalism some have taught, for example, that the Sermon of the Mount (Matt. 5–7) has no relevance to the believer today. For example, Chafer places the Sermon on the Mount under his discussion of "The Teachings of the Kingdom" in which he states, "The teachings of the kingdom presented in Matthew 5–7 are in exact accord with the Old Testament predictions regarding the kingdom, and are almost wholly in disagreement with the teachings of grace."[60] This perspective of the Sermon on the Mount was based upon the view that the purpose of the sermon was to provide the "constitution" for the coming earthly kingdom.[61] Since that kingdom has been postponed, the conclusion is that the sermon does not apply to the present dispensation.

However, though the language of the sermon is couched in terms that both anticipate the kingdom as well as reflect the life of believers under the law (namely, the very Jewish disciples who first heard the sermon), the vast majority of dispensationalists today would affirm the applicability of the principles, if not many of the specific teachings, found in the sermon. For example, no one today should disagree with Jesus' interpretation of the law (5:21–48), His exposition of the proper way to practice almsgiving, prayer and fasting (6:1–18) or His admonitions concerning money and worry (6:19–34). What is more, some of Jesus' instructions in the sermon are incongruous with life as it will be experienced during the millennial kingdom—as the Bible prophesies elsewhere. Examples of this include warnings against persecution (5:10–12) and the instruction to pray for the coming kingdom (6:10). As one dispensational scholar states, the sermon is:

> ...*primarily* addressed to disciples exhorting them to a righteous life in view of the coming kingdom. Those who were not genuine disciples were warned concerning the danger of their hypocrisy and unbelief.[62]

Likewise, Ryrie argues that the sermon "relates to any time that the kingdom is offered. And . . . is applicable and profitable to believers in this age."[63]

A final objection to dispensationalism worth considering is that some believe that "these characteristics seem to dissect history and compartmentalize its eras" into arbitrary periods that seemingly have no logical relationship to one another.[64] However, there is a continuity and a coherency of principles from one dispensation to the next, such as the basis and means of salvation and the objective of God's glory. There is also a sense of progress as God inexorably brings history to its climatic conclusion. As one dispensationalist puts it, "The dispensations are not simply . . . *different* arrangements between God and humankind, but . . . *successive* arrangements in the progressive revelation and accomplishment of redemption."[65] And yet another dispensationalist writes:

> A fresh Divine beginning is never merely a return to the old. In each reformation born out of collapse lay at the same time the seed of a life-program for the future. . . . In the sphere of the Bible, as elsewhere, there is an ascent from lower to higher, from twilight to clearness.[66]

In summary, while a few of the objections against dispensational teaching have some basis in history, they are today largely strawmen with no validity. This is not to say that everyone is convinced of the truth of dispensationalism. But what often passes as legitimate criticism of dispensationalism today is frequently based upon outdated conceptions of dispensationalism that few, if any, modern dispensationalists hold.

Discussion Questions

1. How strong do you regard the argument that the newer an idea the less trustworthy it is?

2. What evidence is there in Scripture that the basis and means of salvation has always been the same in every dispensation?

3. What elements of previous dispensations can you identify as still being in force today?

4. What, if any, aspects of dispensational teaching do you find difficult to square with your present understanding of Scripture? How might you seek to reconcile this conflict?

CHAPTER 9:

SO WHAT?

The Benefits of Dispensationalism

As we conclude this brief survey of dispensationalism, we have seen that God has had a specific purpose in each dispensation whereby humanity has been tested with regard to some means of living righteously before God. Each time people have failed to live in accord with God's expectations, even when they have been given special promises and Divine resources. However, with each failure, God has graciously provided a means of redemption, culminating in the greatest revelation of grace and redemption of all, the Lord Jesus Christ. Also, through all of these successive dispensations, God has been and will be glorified, which is the ultimate reason for all that He does in this world and in the lives of those He created and loves. At the same time, He is at work to redeem "an innumerable company" (Heb. 12:22) from every nation so that they can enjoy Him forever "with joy unspeakable" (1 Pet. 1:8, KJV). To this great task He calls His church to dedicate itself diligently and cheerfully.

At this point a natural question that may arise is: so what? What difference does it make whether one holds to a dispensational approach to Scripture or some other approach? Well, on the one hand, the position you hold will not make too much of a difference in the way you live your life on a day-to-day basis. Whether you are a dispensationalist or not, you still need to "'love the LORD your God with all your heart, with all your soul, with all your strength, and with all your mind,' and 'your neighbor as yourself'" (Luke 10:27). You also need to be part of the "ambassadors for Christ" wherever you are (2 Cor. 5:20), and you need to seek to "do all to the glory of God" (1 Cor. 10:31).

On the other hand, there are several benefits to the dispensational approach that can positively impact your life and ministry. First, dispensationalism helps us to make sense of the Bible. The framework of the seven dispensations helps us to better understand the progress of God's revelation as we work through the various books of the Bible. Dispensationalism enables us to see the major changes and developments that take place between the testaments as well as between major sections of the book of Genesis, which comprises the first four dispensations. Finally, dispensationalism helps us to better understand God's purposes in the world today and our expected role within those purposes.

Second, dispensationalism helps us to avoid misapplying Scripture. Without the dispensational framework, one is less sure as to what responsibilities today's Christians hold before God. For some non-dispensational traditions, there is a sense in which the Christian is still under some obligation to obey the law, even though Scripture makes it clear that the believer is no longer under the law (Rom. 7:4–6; Gal. 5:18). This leads to confusion wherein some, for example, believe they must observe Sabbatarian restrictions. Thus, a dispensational perspective has some real bearing upon how the Christian life is lived, and this is an eminently practical consideration.

Third, dispensationalism provides real hope and comfort for Christians as well as greater motivation for holiness in life. The dispensational perspective of the last days teaches that the believer can expect the imminent return of Christ (otherwise known as a pretribulational rapture). This truth is of far more comfort than the non-dispensational teaching that believers must experience the tribulation period before the return of Jesus (otherwise known as a posttribulational rapture). Also, a pretribulational rapture tends to promote purity of life through a readiness to meet the Lord at any moment. Not surprisingly, one of the key rapture texts is imbedded within exhortations to holiness in life (Tit. 2:11–14). In addition, dispensationalists can provide hope and comfort for Jews as they affirm a future for national Israel, which can aid the gospel witness to Jews who are looking for the coming Messiah.[67]

Fourth, as mentioned in the introduction, dispensationalism provides a cogent and satisfying perspective of the course of human history. What was destroyed and corrupted in the garden of Eden within human history will be restored as well within human history. The Lord will be vindicated and glorified through all that has transpired upon earth, and this glory will resonate through those who were redeemed by Christ for all eternity.

Discussion questions

1. Which one of the benefits of dispensationalism described above is most meaningful to you and why?

2. How does a dispensational understanding of Christ's return promote holiness of lifestyle?

3. How convinced are you of the dispensational understanding of Scripture? What do you consider to be its strongest arguments? Its weakest?

4. How prepared do you feel to explain dispensationalism to someone? What can you do to become better prepared?

BENEFITS TO THE DISPENSATIONAL APPROACH

Dispensationalism helps us to make sense of the Bible.

Dispensationalism helps us to avoid misapplying Scripture.

Dispensationalism provides real hope and comfort for Christians as well as greater motivation for holiness in life.

Dispensationalism provides a cogent and satisfying perspective of the course of human history.

APPENDIX 1:

A CASE FOR PRETRIBULATIONALISM

The term *rapture* refers to a future event in which all believers who have lived during the dispensation of grace will be resurrected and united with Christ forever (John 14:1–3, 1 Cor. 15:51–52; 1 Thess. 4:13–18). On this, all Christians essentially agree. However, there is great debate over the *timing* of this event. In this regard, there are three primary views.[68] All three relate to a future period known as the tribulation, a seven–year period of unprecedented persecution and Divine judgment (Matt. 24:3–27; cf. Dan. 9:24–27).

Pretribulationalism holds that the rapture is a separate event from the visible coming of Christ in glory (as described, for example, in Matt. 24:28–31 and Rev. 19:11–16) and will *precede* the tribulation.

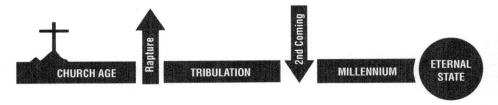

Midtribulationalism maintains, as the name suggests, that the rapture of the church will occur approximately in the middle of the seven–year tribulation period.

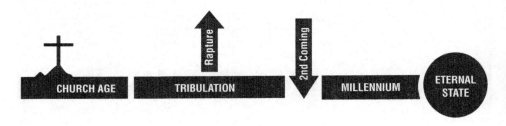

Finally, *posttribulationalism* sees the rapture of the church and the visible return of Christ as essentially one event that will occur near to or at the very end of the tribulation period.

So, does the position one holds make any difference? While godly persons hold to all three positions, the practical impact of each view on the lifestyle of the believer differs and must be considered. There are several lines of argument for a pretribulational rapture of the church.

1. The Argument from Imminence.

The fact that believers are exhorted toward "eagerly waiting" (1 Cor. 1:7) and told to "eagerly wait for" (Phil. 3:20) the coming of Christ suggests an imminent or *any moment* return (cf. Tit. 2:13, 1 Thess. 1:10; Js. 5:7–9; 2 Pet. 3:11–13). Consistent with this truth, Paul seemed to expect that he would be alive when the Lord returned (e.g., 1 Cor. 15:52; 1 Thess. 4:17). If one affirms the truth of Christ's imminent return, then belief in a pretribulational rapture is the most logical position. Conversely, an imminent return is logically inconsistent with any view that insists upon a period of time before the rapture can occur.

2. The Argument from Dissimilarity.

The passages which explicitly speak of the rapture (see above) mention no signs or other events that are elsewhere associated with the visible return of Christ to the earth in glory (Matt. 24:29–31, 2 Thess. 1:7–10; Rev. 19:11–21). In addition, there are several other distinctions between the two *comings*. That is, they differ in place (the clouds vs. the earth), purpose (to rescue the church vs. to judge unrepentant humanity and establish the kingdom) and character (invisible and instantaneous versus visible and progressive). Thus, there is enough dissimilarity between clear rapture and clear second advent passages to warrant the claim that the Bible teaches two distinct events, which will occur at two different times.

Some object that the New Testament writers use the same exact vocabulary to describe both events, suggesting they are one and the same. However, the Old Testament also speaks of two distinct "comings" of the Messiah: one in humility (e.g., Isa. 53) and one in glory (e.g., Zech. 14). Yet, in some prophesies the two comings are intertwined with no obvious intervening time period (e.g. Isa. 61:1–3). Therefore, based upon Old Testament precedent, it is reasonable to postulate a gap of time between these two related but apparently distinct phases of the promised return of Jesus.

3. The Argument from the Nature of the Tribulation Period.

Dispensationalists would argue that the tribulation period pertains primarily to the reconstituted nation of Israel. For example, Jeremiah 30:7 refers to it as "the time of Jacob's trouble." In Daniel's famous prophecy of "seventy weeks" (Dan. 9:24–27) or 70 sets of seven years, each to complete Gods prophetic program for Israel, the *70th week* corresponds to the tribulation period, during which a seven-year covenant between Israel and the Antichrist will be established (Dan. 9:24–27). In addition, Daniel 12:1 speaks of "a time of trouble" during which the nation of Israel "shall be delivered." Finally, as seen in Jesus' description of this future time, there is a distinctly Jewish characteristic to the tribulation period (Matt. 24:15–20).

Another important aspect of the nature of the tribulation is that it will be an unprecedented time of experiencing God's "wrath" (Rev. 6:15–17; cf. 2 Thess. 1:7–8). However, true believers in Jesus are explicitly promised *exclusion* from God's future "wrath" (1 Thess. 1:10; 5:1–9). As Jesus Himself tells the church at Philadelphia in Asia Minor:

> Because you have kept My command to persevere, I also will keep you from the hour of trial which shall come upon the whole world, to test those who dwell on the earth. (Rev. 3:10)

This verse is perhaps the most explicit affirmation of a pretribulational rapture in the New Testament.[69] Though some argue that this promise only guarantees that Christians will not suffer the trials God intends for unrepentant humanity, such as He did when He provided protection to Israel prior to the Exodus, the wording of the text is explicit in promising exemption from the time period itself ("the hour of trial"). Thus, the characteristic of the tribulation period as one focused upon the Jewish nation and the expression of God's wrath strongly suggests the absence of the church during this time.

4. Other arguments.

The many Old Testament prophecies of the presence of non-glorified or sinful, aging and mortal persons in the millennial kingdom are yet another argument for a pretribulational rapture (e.g., Isa. 11:3–5, 65:20–21; Zech. 8:3–5, 14:16–21). Evidently, these will be people who will come to faith in Christ during the seven–year tribulation period and will survive until Jesus' return to earth (Matt. 25:31–46). They then will be ushered into the kingdom as redeemed, though mortal, persons who will eventually have children, who will need to be saved through faith in Christ as well. The descendants of these tribulation survivors will ultimately rebel against the Lord at the end of the millennium (Rev. 20:7–9).

However, in order to account for their presence in the millennium, there must be some period of time between the rapture and the visible descent of Christ to the earth. Accordingly, a posttribulational rapture cannot properly account for such persons, because posttribulationalists view the rapture and the second coming of Christ as one event. While a midtribulational view could also explain the presence of these persons, this Biblical fact is a strong argument against posttribulationalism.

The apparent timing of "the marriage supper of the Lamb" (Rev. 19:9; cf. vv. 6-8) also favors a pretribulational rapture. This event takes place in heaven (cf. vv. 1–6) and involves the "bride" (NASB) "of the Lamb" (v. 7), a descriptor elsewhere applied to the church (cf. Eph. 5:22–32; 2 Cor. 11:2). This heavenly event appears to take place prior Christ's visible return to the earth (Rev. 19:11–16). Obviously, the presence of the church in heaven prior to Christ's second coming to earth is consistent with a pretribulational rapture. Also, the fact that all believers will be judged at "the judgment seat of Christ" (2 Cor. 5:10; cf. 1 Cor. 3:10–15;) in heaven, where they will also receive clothing of "fine linen, clean and bright" (Rev. 19:8), implies a pretribulational rapture.

Interestingly, the teaching about the rapture is referred to as "a mystery" (1 Cor. 15:51), which generally refers to the giving of a new "revelation" (Eph. 3:3). But the teaching about Christ's visible return to earth was already well known (Acts 1:11). This strongly suggests that the rapture must be an event that is distinct from Christ's visible return to earth. Also, if God will need to shorten the tribulation period "for the elect's sake," as Jesus prophesied (Matt. 24:22), then it seems odd to argue, as posttribulationalists do, that God will protect the elect during the tribulation. If they will already be protected by God, what need is there to shorten the time period at all?

Finally, the absence of any mention of the church in Revelation 6–18, along with the corresponding images of her in heaven in Revelation 4 and 5, as well as God's use of redeemed Jews to evangelize the world in Revelation 7 and 14, are additional arguments for a pretribulational rapture. A corollary of this absence is the heavy Jewish nature of Revelation 6 to 18. That is, these chapters are saturated with Jewish terminology, a fact consistent with nature of the tribulation as noted above.

Some argue that the teaching of a pretribulational rapture is a recent (19th century) theological innovation, unknown for nearly the first 1,800 years of the church. However, as noted in the chapter on objections to dispensationalism, the test of a teaching is not its age but its fidelity to the Scriptures. Nevertheless, there is an intriguing statement by a little known church father, Ephraem the Syrian (373 AD): *"For all the saints and Elect of God are gathered, prior to the tribulation that is to come, and are taken to the Lord lest they see the confusion that is to overwhelm the world because of our sins."*[70] This statement appears to be in perfect accord with the teaching of a pretribulational rapture. Though similar teachings are difficult to find in church history until the modern era, this citation demonstrates that the concept of a pretribulational rapture had adherents very early in the history of the church.

A concluding argument for pretribulationalism is its practical benefits. First, it provides encouraging and comforting hope to believers (Tit. 2:13; cf. John 14:1; 1 Thess. 4:13, 17). Second, it is a motivation to godly living (Tit. 2:11–14; 2 Pet. 3:11–12). Third, it is a motivation to evangelism (2 Thess. 2:7–12). This is not to say that those who are not pretribulationalists cannot lead godly and evangelistic lives. But the truth of pretribulationalism most naturally lends itself to such Christian virtues.

APPENDIX 2:
PROGRESSIVE DISPENSATIONALISM

Approximately 30 years ago, a theological innovation known as progressive dispensationalism arose within dispensationalism. Since then, dispensational thinking has come to be dominated by this perspective.[71] While there is much upon which traditional dispensationalists and progressive dispensationalists agree, there are some important differences in the realm of hermeneutics or interpretive approach.

According to Darrell Bock, one of the original proponents of progressive dispensationalism, "The dispute [between traditional and progressive dispensationalists] is about the most appropriate way to synthesize vast amounts of biblical material."[72] Specifically, Bock contends that a "complementary relationship" exists between the Old and New Testaments such that "a normal, contextually determined reading often brings concepts from the Hebrew Scriptures together in the New Testament in a way that completes and expounds what was already present in the older portion of God's Word."[73] In this manner, the New Testament produces "fresh associations." Yet, Bock is emphatic that these associations or "additions" are "not at the expense of the original promise" or the meaning of the Old Testament text.[74] Rather, the interpreter must be "sensitive to how the New Testament complements" the Old Testament "by expressing fulfillment today in Christ."[75]

One major result of this interpretative approach is that, according to progressive dispensationalists, Christ is now fulfilling the terms of the Davidic Covenant. Indeed, everything Jesus did during his earthly ministry or does today as the exalted Christ is viewed as an expression of his rule as the Son of David. Thus, Bock regards Christ's baptism with the Spirit, His offer of forgiveness, His calming of the waves and his feeding of the 5,000 as manifestations of his "Davidic authority."[76] Likewise, in the present time, all of Christ's activity is viewed as pouring out "the benefits of his victory, the spoils of His Rule."[77]

Yet, while Christ's Messianic claims were no doubt authenticated by His miraculous deeds, it does not necessarily follow that Davidic authority was the basis of such acts. Also, nowhere is Christ described as the king of the church, reigning over her. Rather, the predominant image is that of Christ as "the head of the body, the church" (Col. 1:18; cf. 1 Cor. 12:12–27; Eph. 1:22–23; 4:4, 12, 15–16; 5:23, 30; Col. 1:24; 2:19). Furthermore, the mediation of the blessings of the New Covenant are clearly a function of Christ's *high priestly* ministry, not his kingly authority (Heb. 4:14–16; 7:21–25; 8:1–6; 12:24).

Practically speaking, progressive dispensationalists maintain that "the messianic work of the exalted Christ in the present . . . provides theological guidance for the mission and vision of the church today."[78] In this regard, they call for an increased emphasis upon social responsibility. Accordingly, Bock rejects the view that the Christian should withdraw from the world, leaving "the secular person to sink in their own mire as society degrades around us, going for change of heart instead."[79] Likewise, another prominent progressive dispensationalist, Craig Blaising, states:

> Christ intends to redeem humankind *socially* as well as individually. *The social redemption of humanity begins in the church.* The righteous society of peoples prophesied under Messiah has begun to appear.[80]

However, the teachings of a reigning Davidic king and the church as a present phase of the eschatological kingdom would seem to lend themselves to the image of a "warrior" church. As such, there exists an implicit danger that some, in their zeal for a "righteous society of peoples," may be tempted to advocate a form of postmillennialism or reconstructionism. One reconstructionist states:

> Personal redemption is not the do-all and end-all of the Great Commission. Thus, our evangelism must include sociology as well as salvation; it must include reform and redemption, culture and

conversion, a new social order as well as a new birth, a revolution as well as a regeneration.[81]

The similarity of this statement with statements by both Blaising and Bock cited above is striking. While Bock rejects the idea that "the mere passage of certain laws or the raw exercise of political clout will improve society," he does advocate calling "transgression sin and seeking to raise the standards of our society," albeit through the simultaneous offer of "God's forgiveness and grace."[82] But this two-pronged definition of the mission of the church in light of the theological emphases of progressive dispensationalism would appear to be but a small step from more aggressive expressions of dominion theology.

Bock admits that the impact of progressive dispensationalism upon the debate between dispensationalists and non-dispensationalists has been to make "a mess of the clean lines of distinction."[83] Indeed, elements of progressive dispensationalism tend to compromise the nature of the church as traditionally understood by dispensationalists as distinct from Israel and God's program for that nation. For example, within progressive dispensationalism, the church is viewed as "an inaugurated form of the future kingdom of God"[84] and a covenant partner "added to Israel as God's covenant people."[85] But this perspective obscures the clear Biblical teaching that the church was a *mystery* in the Old Testament (cf. Eph. 3:3–6). It also has the effect of spiritualizing the Old Testament promises of an earthly kingdom ruled by a literal king in Jerusalem (Isa. 2:2–4; Zech.

14:9–21). Instead, the church should be viewed as "the beneficiary of some of the provisions of the new covenant (2 Cor. 3:4–6) without becoming a covenant partner."[86]

In summary, progressive dispensationalism is a system that in many respects resembles traditional dispensationalism, yet its distinctive teachings open the door to even greater departure from traditional dispensationalism than is presently advocated. For example, in light of the view of the church as a present phase of the coming kingdom, what need is there of a pretribulational rapture? Not surprisingly, Blaising and Bock's comprehensive presentation of progressive dispensationalism relegates discussion of the timing of the rapture to a footnote.[87] And elsewhere Bock states: "For me the blessed hope is not tied to the timing of the event that kicks it off [as much as] to what it represents . . . our transformation and redemption."[88] In addition, the continuance of sign miracles throughout "the 'already' stage of His [Christ's] Davidic reign" can easily be deduced, even as some Pentecostals have already done.[89]

For these reasons and others, progressive dispensationalism must be regarded as more than a mere "development" within dispensationalism.[90] Rather, it is a hybrid of traditional dispensationalism and various contemporary forms of thinking, whose resultant form and implications lack a clear means of maintaining itself within the dispensational fold.

ENDNOTES

1 This point of view is sometimes referred to as *relativism or postmodernism*.

2 All Scripture quotations, unless otherwise indicated, are taken from the New King James Version®. Copyright © 1982 by Thomas Nelson. Used by permission. All rights reserved. A number of other versions are also referenced. See the copyright page for complete information.

3 Literal interpretation also takes into account the historical and culture differences between the world of the Bible and the contemporary world. Background studies concerning the cultures and historical setting of Biblical times as well as studies concerning changes to the meanings of words over time are important to the process of literal interpretation. Thankfully, many excellent tools and resources are available to conduct such studies, especially for the English reader. For this reason, literal interpretation is sometimes referred to as *grammatical-historical interpretation*.

4 The rules of interpretation are collectively referred to as *hermeneutics*, which is the science of interpretation.

5 For example, according to Ryrie, "Classic dispensationalism is a result of consistent application of the basic hermeneutical principle of literal, normal, or plain interpretation. No other system of theology can claim this" (Charles C. Ryrie, *Dispensationalism* [Chicago: Moody, 2007], p. 97).

6 Ryrie, *Dispensationalism*, p. 20. Also, playing off the Greek term (*oikonomia*) often translated "dispensation" in the New testament, he defines a dispensation as "*a distinguishable economy in the outworking of God's purpose*" (Ibid, p. 33).

7 Renald E. Showers, *There Really is a Difference! A Comparison of Covenant and Dispensational Theology* (Bellmawr, NJ: The Friends of Israel Gospel Ministry, Inc., 1990), p. 30. Italics in the original.

8 Some regard the seven-year tribulation period as an eighth dispensation.

9 Ryrie, *Dispensationalism*, p. 34.

10 Louw, J. P., & Nida, E. A., *Greek-English Lexicon of the New Testament: Based on*

Semantic Domains (electronic ed. of the 2nd edition), (New York: United Bible Societies, 1996), Vol. 1, p. 357.

11 The ESV is used here to illustrate the sense of **οἰκονομία** that most closely resembles the theological definition of a dispensation. The NKJV reads "fellowship" based upon a *Textus Receptus* reading of **κοινωνία**.

12 For example, see renowned Reformed theologian Louis Berkhof's discussion in his classic work *Systematic Theology* (Grand Rapids: Wm B. Eerdmans Publishing Co., 1941), pp. 345ff.

13 Ryrie says this distinction constitutes part of the *sine qua non* or "essence of dispensationalism" (*Dispensationalism*, pp. 45-48).

14 See, for example, Paul's explanation in Romans 11:11–32 of God's sovereign purposes in Israel's historical judgment to provide for greater reception of the gospel by the Gentile world in this dispensation. Ultimately, Paul says, Israel "will . . . be grafted into" (v. 24), "and so all Israel will be saved" (v. 26).

15 This approach to the relationship between Israel and the church is also referred to as *supersessionism* or *replacement theology*, in that the church is seen to supersede or replace Israel in the purposes and plan of God

16 Another way to put this is that dispensationalists, while recognizing the progress of revelation over time, insist upon the *priority* of the Old Testament or "the preservation of the literal interpretation of the Old Testament at all points of theologizing in the light of progressive revelation" (Michael Stallard, "Literal Interpretation, Theological Method, and the Essence of Dispensationalism," *The Journal of Ministry and Theology* 1 [Spring 1997]: 35–36).

17 Ryrie, *Dispensationalism*, p. 22.

18 Ibid., p. 21.

19 John F. Walvoord, "Reflections on Dispensationalism," *Bibliotheca Sacra* 158 (April–June 2001): 132.

20 Ryrie, *Dispensationalism*, pp. 40-41.

21 Ibid., p. 41.

22 For a thorough defense of the pretribulational interpretation of this verse, see Jeffrey L. Townsend, "The Rapture in Revelation 3:10." *Bibliotheca Sacra* 137 (July–September 1980): 252–266.

23 We may note in this regard that the doctrine of the trinity is also a theological inference drawn from Scripture.

24 Some, such as Ryrie and Showers, prefer the term "Innocency." See Ryrie, *Dispensationalism*, p. 59; and Showers, *There Really is a Difference!*, p. 33.

25 Ryrie suggests the term *"innocent"* may be "too neutral," because, "Adam was not created merely innocent but with a positive holiness that enabled him to have face-to-face communication with God" (*Dispensationalism*, p. 59).

26 For a thorough defense of the complementarian view of marriage see John Piper and Wayne Grudem, *Recovering Biblical Manhood and Womanhood (Redesign): A Response to Evangelical Feminism* (Wheaton: Crossway, 2012).

27 The Bible seems to imply that Cain and Abel were Adam and Eve's first children, and that may very well have been the case, though we cannot be dogmatic. Interestingly,

based upon most translations of Genesis 4:1, Eve seems to give credit to the Lord for being able to acquire her firstborn son, Cain. However, literally the text reads: "I have gotten a man, from the Lord." Admittedly, this is a somewhat cryptic and therefore difficult statement to translate, but I favor understanding her to say: "I have gotten a man, like the Lord." In other words, like the Lord, she has become a giver of life. So rather than declaring her dependence upon and gratefulness to the Lord, in fact she appears to be boasting in her ability to have obtained that which God had promised He would provide (Gen. 3:15).

28 "The nature of rebellious man unfolds in the person of **Cain** who had an auspicious beginning as the child of hope. But the narrative lines him up with the curse; he **worked the soil** (lit., ground, *ăxāmâh*, Gen. 4:2; cf. 3:17). **Abel**, however, seems to be lined up with man's original purpose, to have dominion over life (cf. 1:28); he **kept flocks**. These coincidental descriptions are enhanced with their actions in worship" (Allen P. Ross, "Genesis" in *The Bible Knowledge Commentary: An Exposition of the Scriptures*. John F. Walvoord & Roy B. Zuck, eds. [Wheaton: Victor Books, 1985], 1:34).

29 Kenneth A. Mathews, *Genesis 1–11:26. The New American Commentary*. Vol. 1a. (Nashville: Broadman & Holman, 1996), p. 270.

30 The Greek translation of the Old Testament Hebrew Scriptures, otherwise, known as the Septuagint version, uses the very familiar New Testament word for grace (*charis*) here to express God's favor toward Noah.

31 The technical term for this figure of speech is an *anthropomorphism*, a quite common phenomenon in the Bible in which human attributes or emotions are attributed to God. Another school of thought, known as open theism, teaches that God really was taken by surprise by this turn of events. But this understanding is far afield of the traditional Christian view of God and creates all sorts of theological problems. For a thorough refutation of open theism, see Millard J. Erickson, *What Does God Know and When Does He Know It?* (Grand Rapids: Zondervan, 2003).

32 In reference to the human ability to make choices, I am well aware of the debate between what is known as *libertarianism* and *compatibilism*, and as an advocate of compatibilistic human freedom, I would maintain that God ultimately desires that people choose Him of their own free will. For further discussion of this issue, see *Predestination and Free Will: Four Views*, ed. David Basinger and Randall Basinger (Downers Grove: InterVarsity, 1986).

33 See "The Cost of Low Fertility in Europe," <http://www.nber.org/digest/jul09/w14820.html>; Internet; accessed 12 March 2016; "Economists fear low birth rates in developed world will choke growth," <http://www.scmp.com/business/economy/article/1510742/economists-fear-low-birth-rates-developed-world-will-choke-growth>; Internet; accessed 12 March 2016.

34 C.S. Lewis, *God in the Dock: Essays on Theology and Ethics* (Grand Rapids: Eerdmans, 1970) p. 292.

35 Some say that to "bear the sword" (v. 4) means merely that government has the right to enforce its laws. But if so, why does Paul use imagery that conveys idea of inflicting harm and even death?

36 The Greek word translated "punishment" (ἐκδίκησις) used by Peter is related to the Greek word "avenger" (ἔκδικος) used in Romans 13:4 and is same word used by Paul to refer to the "vengeance" that belongs only to God in Romans 12:19.

37 For a reasoned defense of capital punishment, see John S. Feinberg & Paul D.

Feinberg, *Ethics for a Brave New World* (Wheaton: Crossway Books, 1993), pp. 127–147.

38 What exactly was Ham's sin of observing Noah's "nakedness" that Shem and Japheth "covered" up (Gen. 9:22, 23)? Ancient Jewish rabbis said Ham castrated Noah. Others claim that Ham committed either sodomy with his father or incest with his mother. Interestingly, in Leviticus 18 Moses uses similar vocabulary: "None of you shall approach anyone who is near of kin to him, to uncover his nakedness: I *am* the LORD. The nakedness of your father or the nakedness of your mother you shall not uncover. She *is* your mother; you shall not uncover her nakedness. The nakedness of your father's wife you shall not uncover; it *is* your father's nakedness." (Lev. 18:6–8). So "uncovering nakedness" is a euphemism for sexual relations or incest, which suggests that Ham committed an act of incest. However, the text says Noah "uncovered himself" (Gen. 9:21, NASB). Most likely, then, Ham gawked at his father's literal nakedness and then reveled in this shameful news by sharing it with his brothers. Whatever the exact nature of Ham's sin, both Shem and Japheth are very careful not to repeat it, and show the utmost respect for their father even after he has brought shame upon himself.

39 The site of ancient Ur is on the banks of the Euphrates River a little more than 100 miles west of the Persian Gulf. "The modern site is known as Tell el Muqayyar, 'The Mound of Bitumen.' The results of archaeological investigations demonstrate that Abraham came from a great city, cultured, sophisticated, and powerful. The landscape was dominated by the ziggurat, or temple tower, and the life of the city was controlled by a religion with a multiplicity of gods" (Walter A. Elwell & Philip W. Comfort, eds. *Tyndale Bible Dictionary* [Wheaton: Tyndale House Publishers, 2001], p. 1,281).

40 Evidently, though Abraham was told to leave behind his family (Gen. 12:1), his father Terah and his nephew Lot traveled with him "as far as Haran" (Gen. 11:31, NASB), where "Terah died" (Gen. 11:32). Then the rest of the family, along with an entourage of servants, journeyed to Canaan (Gen. 12:4–5).

41 Some, such as Ryrie (*Dispensationalism*, p. 61), refer to this dispensation as the "*Dispensation of Patriarchal Rule.*" However, the patriarchs did not rule so much as they sojourned in the Promised Land, in anticipation of the fulfillment of God's promises (cf. Heb. 11:13).

42 According to Genesis 15:18, God specifies that Israel's territory would extend "from the river of Egypt to the great river, the River Euphrates." However, Israel has never fully possessed all of this territory, even at its greatest geopolitical extent under Solomon. As Constable explains 1 Kings 4:21: "Solomon's domain stretched from **the** Euphrates **River** (cf. v. 24) on the east and north **to the land of the Philistines** on the west and **Egypt** to the southwest. This does not mean that the Abrahamic Covenant was fulfilled in Solomon's day (Gen. 15:18–20), for not all this territory was incorporated into the geographic boundaries of Israel; many of the subjected kingdoms retained their identity and territory but paid taxes (**tribute**) to Solomon. Israel's own geographic limits were 'from Dan to Beersheba' (1 Kings 4:25)" (Thomas L. Constable, "1 Kings" in *The Bible Knowledge Commentary: An Exposition of the Scriptures.* John F. Walvoord and Roy B. Zuck, eds. [Wheaton: Victor Books, 1985], 1:496–497).

43 Recent authors argue that the land promise as well as the covenant made with the patriarchs have been fulfilled "typologically" in Christ (See Peter J. Gentry and Stephen J. Wellum, *Kingdom through Covenant: A Biblical-Theological Understanding of the Covenants* [Wheaton: Crossway, 2012]). Gentry and Wellum see their proposal

as a *via media* between dispensationalism and covenant theology (Ibid., p. 12). Similarly, Martin argues for a typological fulfillment of the land promises (Oren R. Martin, *Bound for the Promised land: The Land Promise in God's Redemption Plan* [Downers Grove: InterVarsity, 2015], p. 17). Martin insists he is not reinterpreting, spiritualizing or contravening the Old Testament promises made to the patriarchs (Ibid., p. 168). However, at the end of the day, a literal understanding of fulfillment has to be set aside. Indeed, many New Testament texts anticipate a literal fulfillment of the land promise as well as a future kingdom on earth as declared repeatedly in the Old Testament prophets (e.g. Matt. 19:28; Lk. 22:16, 18, 30; Acts 1:6, 3:20–21, 15:15–17, Rom. 11:25–32).

44 "To the question 'Why then the law?' [Galatians 3:19a] . . . two answers are given: (i) to multiply (and even to stimulate) transgressions; (ii) to confine all in the prison-house of sin, from which there is no exit but the way of faith" (F. F. Bruce, *The Epistle to the Galatians: A Commentary on the Greek Text* [Grand Rapids: Eerdmans, 1982], p. 175).

45 "Dispensationalists . . . sometimes make such hard and fast distinctions between the ages and characteristics of the various dispensations that they . . . have said very little about grace in the Old Testament" (Ryrie, *Dispensationalism*, pp. 37-38).

46 "The physical and national aspects of the New Covenant which pertain to Israel have not been appropriated to the church. Those are yet to be fulfilled in the Millennium. The church today shares in the soteriological aspects of that covenant, established by Christ's blood for all believers" (D. K. Lowery, "2 Corinthians" in *The Bible Knowledge Commentary* [Wheaton: Victor Books, 1985]: 2:560–561).

47 Arguments that seek to spiritualize this number as some undefined period of time or to equate it with the present church age flounder upon the shoals of normal hermeneutics. See Jack Deere, "Premillennialism in Revelation 20:4–6," *Bibliotheca Sacra* 135 (January–March 1978): 58–73; and Jeffrey Townsend, "Is the Present Age the Millennium?" *Bibliotheca Sacra* 140 (July–September 1983): 206–221.

48 Millard J. Erickson, *Contemporary Options in Eschatology* (Grand Rapids: Baker Book House, 1977), p. 111.

49 Showers, *There Really is a Difference!*, p. 28.

50 Ibid.

51 Mark Galli and Ted Olsen, eds. *131 Christians Everyone Should Know* (Nashville: B&H Publishing Group, 2000), pp. 99–100.

52 Timothy P. Weber, s.v., "Dispensationalism," in *Dictionary of Christianity in America*, Daniel G. Reid, Robert D. Linder, Bruce L. Shelley and Harry S. Stout, eds. (Downers Grove, IL: InterVarsity Press, 1990).

53 Ed. C.I. Scofield (New York: Oxford, 1917).

54 Ed. Charles Caldwell Ryrie (Chicago: Moody Press, 1994).

55 See *The Scofield Reference Bible*, ed. C.I. Scofield (New York: Oxford, 1917), p. 1,115, note 2. Under the heading "Justification," Chafer makes this statement: "A distinction must be observed here between just men of the Old Testament and those justified according to the New Testament. According to the Old Testament men were just because they were true and faithful in keeping the Mosaic Law . . . whereas New Testament justification is God's work for man in answer to faith (Rom. 5:1)" (Lewis Sperry Chafer, *Systematic Theology*, vols. 1–8 [Dallas: Dallas Seminary Press, 1947], 7:219). Yes, under the heading "Salvation," he quotes two Old Testament texts and

states: "Any system which tends to combine human responsibility with this divine undertaking is wrong" (Ibid., 7:273).

56 Ryrie, *Dispensationalism*, p. 134, emphasis in original.

57 Charles Hodge, *Systematic Theology* (Grand Rapids: Eerdmans, 1946), 2:372–373, emphasis added. Quoted in Ryrie, *Dispensationalism*, p. 132.

58 Ibid.

59 J. Barton Payne, *An Outline of Hebrew History* (Grand Rapids: Baker, 1954), p. 222, emphasis added. Cited in Ryrie, *Dispensationalism*, p. 132.

60 Chafer, *Systematic Theology*, 4:214.

61 Scofield states that the Sermon on the Mount "gives the divine constitution for the righteous government of the earth. . . . In this sense the Sermon on the Mount is pure law . . . in its primary application [it] gives neither the privilege nor the duty of the Church" (*The Scofield Reference Bible*, ed. C.I. Scofield [New York: Oxford, 1917], p. 1,000). On the other hand, Scofield also affirms, "There is a beautiful moral application to the Christian . . . [its] principles fundamentally reappear in the teaching of the Epistles" (Ibid.).

62 Stanley D. Toussaint, *Behold the King: A Study of Matthew* (Grand Rapids: Kregel, 1980), p. 94, emphasis in original. More recently Thomas opines: "The Sermon on the Mount was . . . an elaboration on what the repentance of Israelites (cf. Matt 3:2, 7, 8; 4:17) would entail if they wanted to qualify to enter that promised Kingdom (Robert L. Thomas, "How to Preach the Sermon on the Mount to a Christian Audience." Unpublished paper presented at the Fifth Council on Dispensational Hermeneutics, October 3–4, 2012).

63 Ryrie, *Dispensationalism*, p. 114.

64 Ibid., p. 42.

65 Craig A. Blaising and Darrell L. Bock, *Progressive Dispensationalism* (Wheaton: Bridgepoint, 1993), p. 48 (emphasis in original).

66 Erich Sauer, *The Dawn of World Redemption* (Grand Rapids: Eerdmans, 1951), p. 54. Cited in Ryrie, *Dispensationalism*, p. 44.

67 Another distinctive of dispensational teaching—and one which non-dispensationalists take dispensationalists to task over—is the insistence upon two distinct *hopes* or *futures* for the church and Israel. For the church, the hope is a *heavenly* one through the coming of the Lord Jesus Christ to receive his bride to himself and bring her to a heavenly abode He has prepared for her (John 14:1–3; 1 Thess. 1:10; Tit. 2:13). On the other hand, the hope of the nation of Israel is an earthly one with their long-awaited Messiah coming to rule over them and the earth from Jerusalem. With regard to God's purposes *in history*, these two "hopes" should be kept distinct (Gary L. Nebeker, "The Theme of Hope in Dispensationalism," *Bibliotheca Sacra* 158 [January–March 2001]: 12). With regard to God's purposes *in eternity*, these two hopes will be merged in the New Jerusalem upon "a new earth" (Rev. 21:1ff). Note that the New Jerusalem assumes the title formerly accorded to the church: "the bride, the Lamb's wife" (v. 9). Note also that, on the one hand, the "twelve gates" leading into the city display "*the names* of the twelve tribes of the children of Israel" (v. 12). On the other hand, "the names of the twelve apostles of the Lamb" are upon the "twelve foundations" for "the wall of the city" (v. 14). Thus, in this description of

eternity we see a merging or conflation of the two historic hopes into one hope for all eternity, though the *memory* of the two historic *peoples of God* is still maintained.

68 A fourth view, called the *partial rapture theory*, postulates that only those believers living lives worthy of the Lord at the time of his coming will be raptured. Few maintain this position today. Yet another view, called the *pre-wrath rapture*, is but a modification of typical posttribulational arguments. For a through exposition and critique of this position from a pretribulational perspective, see Renald E. Showers, *The Pre-Wrath Rapture View: An Examination and Critique* (Grand Rapids: Kregel Publications, 2001).

69 As noted in the introduction, for a through defense of the pretribulational interpretation of this verse, see Jeffrey L. Townsend, "The Rapture in Revelation 3:10." *Bibliotheca Sacra* 137 (July-September 1980): 252–266.

70 Timothy J. Demy and Thomas D. Ice, "The Rapture and an Early Medieval Citation," *Bibliotheca Sacra* 152 (July-September 1995): 306–317.

71 A notable exception would be the Baptist Bible Seminary in Clarks Summit, Pa., where I earned my doctor of philosophy degree.

72 Darrell L. Bock, "Hermeneutics of Progressive Dispensationalism," in *Three Central Issues in Contemporary Dispensationalism: A Comparison of Traditional and Progressive Views*, ed. Herbert W. Bateman IV (Grand Rapids: Kregel, 1999), p. 86.

73 Bock, "Hermeneutics of Progressive Dispensationalism," p. 89.

74 Craig A. Blaising and Darrell L. Bock, ed., "Dispensationalism, Israel and the Church: Assessment and Dialogue," in *Dispensationalism, Israel and the Church: The Search for Definition* (Grand Rapids: Zondervan, 1992), pp. 392-393.

75 Bock, "Hermeneutics of Progressive Dispensationalism," p. 93.

76 Darrell L. Bock, "Covenants in Progressive Dispensationalism," in *Three Central Issues in Contemporary Dispensationalism*, ed. Herbert W. Bateman IV (Grand Rapids: Kregel, 1999), pp. 198, 200.

77 Darrell L. Bock, "The Son of David and the Saints' Task: The Hermeneutics of Initial Fulfillment," *Bibliotheca Sacra* 150 (October-December 1993): 454.

78 Bock, "Hermeneutics of Progressive Dispensationalism," p. 94.

79 Darrell L. Bock, "Why I Am a Dispensationalist with a Small 'd'," *Journal of the Evangelical Theological Society* 41:3 (September 1998): 394.

80 Blaising and Bock, *Progressive Dispensationalism*, p. 287 (emphasis in original).

81 George Grant, *Bringing in the Sheaves* (Atlanta: American Vision Press, 1985), p. 70. Cited by H. Wayne House and Thomas Ice, *Dominion Theology: Blessing or Curse?* (Portland: Multnomah, 1988), p. 150.

82 Bock, "Small 'd'," p. 394.

83 Bock, "Small 'd'," p. 388.

84 Blaising and Bock, *Progressive Dispensationalism*, p. 286.

85 Elliott E. Johnson, "Response" to Darrell L. Bock, "Covenants in Progressive Dispensationalism, in *Three Central Issues in Contemporary Dispensationalism*, ed. Herbert W. Bateman IV (Grand Rapids: Kregel, 1999), p. 210.

86 Johnson, "Response" to "Covenants in Progressive Dispensationalism," p. 206.

87 Blaising and Bock, *Progressive Dispensationalism*, p. 264. In footnote 15, Blaising states the somewhat uncertain conclusion that the rapture "would appear to be pretribulational."

88 Bock, "Small 'd'," p. 395.

89 Ryrie, *Dispensationalism*, p. 208. For example, Oss cites Bock's "The Reign of the Lord Christ" to argue the continuance of the gifts (Douglas A. Oss, "A Pentecostal/Charismatic View," in *Are Miraculous Gifts for Today?* ed. Wayne A. Grudem [Grand Rapids: Zondervan, 1996], pp. 268–269).

90 See Craig A. Blaising, "Development of Dispensationalism by Contemporary Dispensationalists," *Bibliotheca Sacra* 145 (July-September 1988): 254–280.

SUBJECT INDEX

SCRIPTURE INDEX

Dispensational Publishing House is striving to become the go-to source for Bible-based materials from the dispensational perspective.

Our goal is to provide high-quality doctrinal and worldview resources that make dispensational theology accessible to people at all levels of understanding.

Visit our blog regularly to read informative articles from both known and new writers.

And please let us know how we can better serve you.

Dispensational Publishing House, Inc.
Taos, NM.

DispensationalPublishing.com

—LEE AND JENNY—

CPSIA information can be obtained
at www.ICGtesting.com
Printed in the USA
BVOW06s1757200317
478876BV00004BA/5/P

9 781945 774041